George Douglas Campbell Argyll

Crofts and Farms in the Hebrides

Being an account of the management of an island estate for 130 years

George Douglas Campbell Argyll

Crofts and Farms in the Hebrides
Being an account of the management of an island estate for 130 years

ISBN/EAN: 9783337315337

Printed in Europe, USA, Canada, Australia, Japan

Cover: Foto ©ninafisch / pixelio.de

More available books at **www.hansebooks.com**

ACCOUNT OF

THE DUKE

EDINBURGH
DAVID DOUGLAS, CASTLE STREET
1883

LORD NAPIER AND ETTRICK,

CHAIRMAN OF THE ROYAL COMMISSION
(HIGHLANDS AND ISLANDS).

MY LORD,—I deem it my duty to communicate to your Lordship, as chairman of the Royal Commission, some authentic information in respect to my Estates of Tyree and the Ross of Mull, which have been lately visited by your Lordship and your colleagues. *Statement relates to Tyree and Mull estates.*

From documents connected with the management of the estate, we have a tolerably complete account of the population, value, and condition of Tyree, from about the middle of the last century to the present date. It may be of interest to the Commission to know the leading facts. *Tyree.*

Leases of all the principal farms on the Island for the usual term of nineteen years, or occasionally of twenty-two years, were granted at various dates between 1753 and 1762. These Leases of course expired at various corresponding dates between 1772 and 1784. It is towards the end of these Leases, and not at the commencement of them, that we first have really detailed information. They were granted by Archibald, third Duke of Argyll, who succeeded in 1743, but whose busy political life probably prevented him from paying close attention to agricultural affairs. But towards the close of these Leases the Argyll estates were in the hands *Leases of principal farms granted between 1753–1762.*

of my grandfather, Field-Marshal John, fifth Duke of Argyll, who succeeded in 1770, was the first President of the Highland and Agricultural Society, and who spent the latter part of his life almost entirely in agricultural pursuits, and especially in the improvement of the breeds of cattle, which had always been, and still are, one of the principal articles of Highland produce. So early, however, as the years 1767-68-69, in three separate papers, we have very full information, evidently collected with great care, on the statistics of the Island. The total population was then only 1676, of whom only 69 were employed in handicrafts other than agricultural. It is remarkable that there is only one column for " tenants and hinds," showing that many families were on the dividing-line between regular agricultural tenants and labourers, or cottars with small plots of land. The total number of both classes is only 236, and a separate class of cottagers is numbered at only 104 on the whole island. The agricultural tenants properly so called seem to have been 170. It is still more worthy of remark that in this return, although there is a careful estimate of all kinds of agricultural produce, there is no mention of the potato ;—cattle, sheep, and horses,—rye, barley, and oats are the only products noted.

The Leases to which I have referred as granted between 1753 and 1762, the rental of 1767, and the reports of 1768-69, make two facts quite certain. The first is that many of the farms, which at a later period became most lamentably subdivided into very small crofts, were then let to single tenants, several of whom were Highland gentlemen non-resident on the Island. The second fact proved by these documents is

Condition of Tyree about 1770.

Many farms afterwards subdivided were then let to single tenants.

that even the farms which were then let to "sundry
tenants" were so let to a comparatively small number,
who had of course proportionately larger shares, and
these shares, if reckoned at the present value, would
represent small farms quite above the definition of System of crofts
crofts, as that definition has been adopted by the did not then exi:
Commission. That is to say, these farms, or shares in
one farm, would now represent a rent above the £30
line. Thus, for example, the two farms of *Gott* and
Hianish, now representing a rental of £163, are
specially mentioned in the report of 1769 as having
only four persons in possession. These two farms, if
now similarly divided, would therefore represent a
much more substantial class of farms than the crofts
now existing, although these have been much raised
and improved within the last thirty years, by the
operations which I shall subsequently explain to the
Commission. The same observation applies to almost
all the farms which were then let under lease, or from
year to year, to small tenants.

This shows the delusion which is commonly entertained, that the system of very small crofts is an old
one. The truth is that in Tyree at least, and in many
other places, it is not nearly one century old. The same
conclusion is even more apparent when we see in this
rental of 1767 that almost all the farms which at a long
subsequent date became overrun and cut up into miser-
ably small possessions, were then not occupied by small
tenants at all, but by individual lessees, or "tacksmen," as they were called in the Highlands. Among
the farms then held in this way I may specify Balle-
phuil, Balemartine, and Barrapol—all of them farms
which, thirty years ago, had become excessively over-

peopled and subdivided, and which even to this day contain some of the smallest crofts upon the island.

The opinion of the reporters of 1769 on the minimum size of farm which it would be wise to assign to one tenant or family is farther indicated by the recommendations they make that certain farms should be more properly divided. Thus they recommend that the three farms of Kenovar, Barrapol, and Ballemenoch, which had then seventeen tenants, should not in future be held by more than ten. It is curious that these farms are now again held by the same number of crofters which held them in 1769. But this condition of things is the result of the gradual process of re-consolidation which has been pursued during the last thirty years, the same farms having become at one time so subdivided that there were no less than twenty-nine tenants, instead of only ten as recommended by the reporters of 1769.

Small tenants were then destroying their possessions by cropping ground suited only for pasture.

The report of 1769 is farther interesting as containing conclusive evidence on the waste and misuse of the land which the small tenants were then making. Much of the soil of Tyree is almost pure shell sand, which yields a rich and beautiful pasture, full of clovers of several species ; but it is unfit for cropping, and when broken up is very apt to become blowing sand—not only sterile in itself, but liable to overrun and render barren large areas of the surrounding land. By this process two considerable farms have actually been destroyed and lost—the whole area being now as sterile as a snow-drift. The report of 1769 shows that the very poor and very ignorant tenants and sub-tenants who were then in possession were cropping this light sandy land to an injurious and dangerous degree, and recommended the erection of strong dividing dykes, with conditions prohibiting the practice.

Another signal example of the contrast between crofts or small farms as recommended by the skilled and intelligent reporters of 1769 and the miserable possessions which subsequently arose from the improvident habits of subdivision, is furnished by the example of the two farms of Balephuil and Balemartine. *Two farms then held by one tenant, and fit only for ten subdivisions, afterwards occupied by 69 crofters, and still by 30.*

These two farms are mentioned as having been "formerly" held by one tenant, who was at that time the factor or chamberlain : and the reporters recommend that if they are to be divided the total number of divisions should not exceed ten. Yet on these two farms the reckless process of subdivision went on subsequently to such an extent that there were no less than sixty-nine crofters—all of the poorest class. At this moment there are still thirty, which is exactly three times the number which the reporters of 1769 could recommend as enough to live comfortably and profitably on the land.

The next document of importance is dated seven years later—in 1776 ; and it is very instructive. It is *Conditions of leases in 1776.* a draft of "Articles, Conditions, and Regulations to be observed by the Tacksmen who have obtained leases of Farms on the Island of Tyree." It appears from this paper that in Tyree, as elsewhere in the Highlands, the small tenants were still holding and cultivating in what was called "runrig," and is still called in Ireland "rundale," that is to say, under a system of management which is absolutely incompatible with the very first germs of agricultural improvement. The possession of each tenant was divided into innumerable separate little plots of land—none of which remained in his possession for more than a year or a couple of years, the various plots and patches being re-divided each year by lot. It was of course the interest and duty of proprietors to put an end to this system, and by no other agency than proprietary power and right could it have been abolished. Like all ancient and barbarous customs it was clung to most tenaciously, although after a little experience of separate possessions the tenants generally soon acknowledged the superiority of the new system. Accordingly, it was laid down as the first and foremost of the new conditions that "runrig" possession of "corn farms" (arable land) were to be entirely abolished, and every tenant was to occupy (by himself or servants, without subletting) a distinct separate possession, more or less extensive, according to his ability, *not below the extent of a four mail land.*

Runrig system of cultivation then abolished.

Crofts not to be under a " four mail land " in extent.

This last condition is especially interesting, as showing again, in a definite form, the opinion then entertained by the proprietor and his advisers as to the minimum size of farm which would constitute a comfortable living for a tenant. A " mail land" was a division which included four of the smaller divisions called a " soum," and each " soum" represented the grass of one cow, or of two two-year-old cattle, or of five sheep, so that each tenant was to have at least a farm capable of holding 16 cows, or 32 young cattle, or 80 sheep. This is, indeed, a very comfortable little farm, and would generally be rented now at more than £30. In other words, they would not be crofts at all, but would belong to the class of small farms.

Meaning of "mail land."

Another important fact we learn from this paper is that the selection of persons to fill the new farms or

Selection of tenants made by public

crofts was not made arbitrarily by any favouritism, but was settled by public roup. No right of possession either by custom or otherwise was claimed or thought of by any tenant or sub-tenant on the island. They had generally held by Lease for definite periods, or as sub-tenants at will under the individual Tacksmen. The new arrangement was made when the Leases came to an end, and when the proprietor by virtue of the expiry of these Leases came again into full possession of the land. The small tenants were taken bound to build the houses and the march fences between each other at their own expense; and as community of possession could not be abolished upon the common pasture land, as it was now abolished on the arable land, the tenants were taken bound to submit to and observe any regulations laid down by the factor for the "souming," or amount of stock to which each tenant should be limited. The prohibition of ploughing up the sandy land, or links, completed the principal regulations which were laid down, and which sufficiently indicate both the wretched husbandry of the preceding times, and the real source from which all improvement came in the times which were to follow.

Two years later, in 1778, a farther report, going in detail into each farm, emphasises the same principles of improvement,—remarks on the poor and scanty kinds of grain which were raised in the Island,— points out that the ignorance of the people was due principally to their total isolation and want of communication with the mainland, and recommends the establishment of regular sailing packet-boats. Notes upon this report, in the Duke's handwriting, make it evident that he had gone minutely into it; and that,

Side notes: roup, and no customary right of possession claimed or thought of by tenants. Conditions of Lease as to houses, common pasture, &c. Report on Island in 1778.

from this date to the end of the century, that is, during the following two-and-twenty years, a great deal had been done in dividing several farms into good-sized separate possessions, and in clearing them of a scattered surplus population, which was transplanted where their labour would be available for agriculture and for fishing. The Duke had then also tried to encourage the fisheries, by keeping men in his own employment; but this was a failure, as the men, being independent of success, were idle and drunken. The reporter, wishing to go out in a boat to try the fishing, had found the Duke's fishermen so drunk that they could not take him. I mention this circumstance, which occurred now more than a century ago, because it enables me to record the fact of a signal change for the better in the habits of the people. The fishermen of Tyree are now as sober as they are industrious. Indeed, I question whether there is any part of the Highlands where drunkenness is less common—a result to which I hope and believe that I have contributed something in never having granted a site for any public-house to be established on the Island.

In the Leases given by the Duke, from 1776 onwards, I find that the erection of houses, and of march fences in the form of dikes, was made an obligation on the tenants themselves, and that this kind of improvement was therefore done under specific agreement that it was to be held as done for valuable consideration received in the Lease, and in the moderate rent offered and accepted. These Leases are farther remarkable for the proof they afford, if, indeed, any proof were needed, that it was solely by the influence

Habits of the fishermen then and now.

Improving Leases granted in 1776 and later.

and authority of the proprietor that various old barbarous habits of cultivation, or rather of waste, were
abolished and abandoned, such as burning of the surface, and others, the very names of which are now
obsolete and forgotten.

This appears to be the proper place to notice the
rise of the trade in kelp, manufactured by the burning Kelp trade.
of drift and cut seaweed—a product which began to be
valuable about the middle of the last century. It is
not, however, till we come to the report of 1778 that
any specific mention is made of the kelp trade. But
in that report the quantity of kelp which could be
produced on the shores of several farms, on an average, Amount produced
is mentioned in the report on these farms. The in 1778 inconsiderable.
amount, however, mentioned is very inconsiderable,
and it is evident that the returns from kelp had not
at that time become any large part of the value of the
Island. But towards the close of the century, and on But towards close
to 1810–12, the produce of the Island in kelp very of century and on
to 1812, produce
often exceeded the whole agricultural rental ; and the often exceeded
system which seems to have been adopted as regards agricultural rental.
the price paid to the tenants of the farms on the shores
of which the kelp was produced, is perhaps the most
important fact which helps to explain the subsequent
economic condition of the people. So large a share in
the price of the kelp seems to have been allowed to
the tenants, and to have been accepted from them to Tenants often paid ·
account of their rents, that very often they had no their whole rent
from produce of
rent at all to pay for their purely agricultural posses- kelp.
sions. In the years from 1800 to 1808, for example,
the island seems to have produced somewhere from
200 to 300 tons of kelp, which in the later part
of this period became worth from £10 to £12 per

ton. After deducting all expenses, this quantity
yielded a sum nearly equal, or sometimes exceeding, the whole agricultural rental ; and in the estate
accounts the factor is found discharging himself of
that rental altogether by setting off against it the
return of kelp. I have letters and papers written by my
grandfather, in which he points out that under these
conditions the tenants had their land practically rent
free, and concludes from this circumstance, and from
his knowledge of the stock and crop raised in the
Rental below true value of land. Island, that the rental must have been, even then, far
below the real value of the land. The indisputable
facts upon which he founded this conclusion were
mainly these—that whereas the whole rental of the
Island was then about £1000, there were not less
than 13,000 acres of fertile land out of which that
rental could be met, without taking into account at
all the very large sum made by the tenants out of
their share of the kelp. The Island was even then
known to produce 1000 bolls of barley. This, together with the kelp, would produce far more than
the whole rent. "I allow," said the Duke, in explaining his calculation, "all the oats, all the potatoes,
all the lint, all the sheep, all the milk, butter, cheese,
poultry, eggs, fish, &c., which in other countries are
sold to contribute rent—I allow all these to go for
the support of the tenants, because I wish them to
live plentifully and happily."

Result in increase of population and reckless subdivision of crofts. It is quite needless to point out the natural and
inevitable consequence of such a condition of things.
If it were possible by the artificial cheapening of com-
modities to establish among any people a higher
standard of living than that to which they were ac-

customed, this benevolence might have been successful. But it is not possible. The establishment of higher standards of living must come by exertion, and by thrift,—not by gratuitous benefits which dispense with both. Accordingly this unnatural lowering of rent, by allowing a wholly extraneous produce to stand in lieu of it,—and all this consequent temporary abundance had the reverse effect. It did not produce wealth or comfort, but, on the contrary, only poverty and indigence. It removed every check upon the law under which population tends to press upon the limits of subsistence. It supplied an insuperable temptation and encouragement to an improvident multiplication of the people, to wasteful habits, and to a systematic breach of the conditions against the reckless subdivision of farms or crofts. When it is remembered further that the period I have now reviewed was contemporary with the introduction and spread of the potato, and of inoculation, which put an end to the old ravages of smallpox, we can readily understand the results which followed.

Accordingly, we find that the population of the Island, which so late as 1769 had only amounted to 1676 persons, had in 1802 multiplied to a total of 2776. And the same rate of multiplication was then going on, and was even rising. The parish registers have been lost up to 1784. But from that year (inclusive) to the end of the century, we have a list of the yearly births and of the yearly marriages. The births in the year 1800 were 116, and the marriages were 41. The last is a far higher rate of marriages to population than now prevails in the most thriving cities of the country.

It is in a paper of a little later date—1802—that we have by far the most able and detailed account of the agriculture of Tyree, and the most vivid picture of the condition to which by over-population and subdivision the inhabitants were then reduced. This Report was drawn up by Mr. Maxwell of Aros—a gentleman whose name was widely known in the first quarter of the present century as my grandfather's chamberlain on his estates in Mull and Morvern. It was in his house at Aros that the many distinguished men in literature and in science who came to visit Staffa and Iona were hospitably received, and were forwarded on the journey by which alone at that time those Islands could be approached. His name is linked with a distinguished man and a distinguished family of our own time—for Mr. Maxwell became the grandfather of the late Dr. Norman Macleod, through a daughter whose most beautiful and venerable old age of nearly one hundred years came to its close but a very short time ago. Mr. Maxwell's Report to my grandfather in 1802 is a model of what may be called the scientific treatment of such a subject. He shows

that there were then 319 tenants of crofts so small that even under better management they were inadequate to support a family, whilst under the wretched husbandry which actually prevailed, they were, of course, still more incapable of doing so.

Many of these crofts barely fed two cows, and an extravagant number of horses reduced the grazing of these cows almost to the starvation point. One consequence was that the cows did not produce a calf above once in two or three years, so that they afforded little profit to the tenants "either in the way of milk or rearing." But this was not all. Preying upon the tenants of these small possessions there was besides a whole host of cottars who had no land of their own, —but who, nevertheless, kept cattle and horses for the collection and transport of sea-weed, and these cattle and horses being wholly unrestrained by adequate fences, impoverished still more the common pasture, and must have trespassed continually even on the crofts themselves. Very naturally, Mr. Maxwell denounced this condition of things as a "shameful abuse and oppression upon the tenants, hampered as they themselves were for want of room." Everything else was of a piece. The barley raised upon the Island is described as "of the meanest quality:" and it appears from many passages of the correspondence of this time, that it had been largely used for illicit distillation. From a careful calculation of the maximum produce of the crofts. consisting of "one mail land," it is shown that, allowing only about one-sixth part for rent, the remaining five-sixths could not support the tenants "except in penury." Mr. Maxwell pointed out the great difficulties in the way of remedying a state of things so desperate,—difficulties increased tenfold by the mental condition of the people. "It is proper," he says, "to remark to your Grace that the general poverty of the tenants, in consequence of the practice of breaking down their possessions into inconsiderable shares—their stubborn attachment to old customs—the idleness of their habits—and their total ignorance of any better system of management, oppose very arduous obstacles to the improvement of the Island." Not that Mr. Maxwell had any doubt of its great

Large number of cottars.

Difficulty of remedying desperate state of affairs.

Suggestion of introducing practical farmer to Island.

natural fertility, for he suggests among other things that some regularly bred and practical farmer should be introduced into the Island to show the people that the soil on which they were only saved from starving by the extraneous resources of the kelp trade was "capable of producing returns of which they had no conception." He pointed out, however, that even this measure would be necessarily slow in its operation, since "the general poverty of their circumstances conspired with the general idleness of their habits and the backwardness of their knowledge," to render hopeless the possibility of such examples being followed.

Necessity of no less than 1000 people emigrating.

Mr. Maxwell had no doubt of the necessity of at least one remedy. He declared his opinion that not less than one thousand people should be assisted to emigrate to America or Canada. The people themselves had come to wish it. My grandfather, though averse, had also come to entertain the proposal. But just at that time one of these panics had arisen about the evils of emigration and depopulation which seem to be of periodical recurrence. A committee of the Highland and Agricultural Society, of which my grandfather was president, had sat upon the subject. They had treated emigration as a national calamity. They had recommended every conceivable expedient—each one more absurd than another—for preventing the people from seeking a land of greater abundance. They had advised the making of roads by Government—the making of canals by Government—the establishment of Government bounties upon fishing—bounties upon building villages—bounties upon crofting — bounties upon building boats — bounties upon anything and everything that could be thought of as bribes and baits to induce the swarming multitudes not to swarm, and not to establish new hives. Under the pressure of this panic, Parliament had been induced to interpose obstacles on emigration by artificial regulations and restraints. My grandfather also was under pressure from different directions. In order to constitute proper crofts it was absolutely necessary to dispossess many families who had squatted on minute subdivisions. He desired also to give land to many fishermen. And last, perhaps not least, the military instincts of the old Field-Marshal made him desirous of accommodating some discharged soldiers of the "Fencible Regiments" which had been raised under him. For all these three classes of men, therefore, he desired to constitute crofts on the plan which he had long contemplated—crofts, if possible, of not less than "four mail lands." *Parliament interposed obstacles to emigration.*

It seems to have been to meet this condition of things that my grandfather John, the fifth Duke, agreed to divide some farms, hitherto let to single tenants; and in 1803 Balemartine was let to thirty-eight crofters, whilst no less than fifty-six applicants are mentioned in one of his notes as anxious to be provided for out of other farms in a similar manner. These crofts, however, seem to have been of a tolerable size, from eight to ten acres. *Farms divided into crofts in 1803 in consequence of increase in population.*

It does not appear that my grandfather had present to his mind the danger of the course he was pursuing. He had indeed some misgivings. But nobody at that time could foresee the scientific discoveries, and the changes in tariffs, &c., which within a few years were to put an end to the large profits derived by the tenantry, as well as by proprietors, from the manufacture of kelp; *Danger of the course not foreseen.*

B

nor did he, perhaps, sufficiently consider that even if that manufacture had continued on the same scale, the increase of population, if not somehow checked, would soon overtake its supplies : and that unless his successors enforced strictly the prohibitions against subdivision, the inevitable result would be a vast semi-pauper population.

These dates are, however, interesting and important, as showing how unfounded are the impressions now common among the people as to the antiquity of their occupation of the small crofts which many of them still possess. In Tyree the great majority of these crofts were not more than about forty years old when the crash of the potato famine came in 1846. And so far from the possessions held by the tenants having long belonged to themselves or their " ancestors," these possessions were either given to them by the special favour of the proprietor at a very recent period, or were still later acquired by irregular subdivisions against the rules and regulations of the estate.

Erroneous impression as to antiquity of small crofts.

All these causes of impoverishment were doubtless aggravated by the death of my grandfather in 1806, and the succession of George, the sixth Duke of Argyll, during whose life of thirty-three years the restraining and regulating power of a landlord was comparatively in abeyance. Nothing but this power, steadily exercised, could have checked the ruinous tendency towards subdivision, or supplied the knowledge and the foresight which are invariably wanting to a population living under such conditions.

After 1806, and during life of sixth Duke, subdivision allowed to go on unchecked.

The result was what might have been expected. Mr. Maxwell of Aros lived to see that result in melancholy operation. Nineteen years after his report to my grandfather, he was again called upon to report to his successor on the condition of Tyree. In 1822 he was obliged to report that, as a "natural consequence" of the system adopted, "the families have now multiplied to such an unmanageable degree that the whole produce of the Island is hardly sufficient for their maintenance, and the crowded population on its surface exhibit in many instances cases of individual wretchedness and misery that perhaps are not to be found in any part of Scotland." The farms which had long been possessed by small tenants were now found to contain 2869 souls, whilst the five farms which had been broken up into small lots now contained no less than 1080. The potato disease was as yet unknown, but the ordinary vicissitudes of the seasons are always at hand to punish glaring departures from sound economic laws. 1821 was a year of extraordinary drought, and on the light sandy soils of Tyree the crops were almost a total failure. The cattle were almost starved, and were so lean as to be unsaleable. Kelp was again the only resource. There was an extraordinary supply of it in 1821. By this means and by wholesale remissions of rent, the crisis was tided over; but no permanent remedy was applied, and so matters went on again in the old rut. In the course of forty-three years from my grandfather's subdivision of the farms,—with little or no increase of agricultural production, and an immense deficit in a manufacturing resource,—the population had nearly doubled, so that when the crash of the potato failure came in 1846 it exceeded 5000 souls, whilst the small crofts had been so much farther subdivided'

Population had nearly doubled in course of 43 years at time of potato failure in 1846.

as to number 380, of whom all but a mere fraction
were below £10 rent, and the great majority (218)
were even below £5. Of these last, again, a very
large number were as low as 30s. and £3. There
were, besides, a large population of cottars who were
without any land, employed, in so far as they worked
at all, in fishing and very casual labour.

Great destitution
of people in 1846.

When the potato famine came in 1846, the destitution of the people was as severe as under such circumstances it could not fail to be. Not only was there
great distress, but there was danger of actual starvation. My father, John, seventh Duke of Argyll, was
then in possession of the estate; but as he was in
feeble health, I was obliged to take a principal share in

Present Duke re-
sponsible for man-
agement since
1846.

devising measures of relief, and as he died in the spring
of the following year, 1847, I consider myself practically responsible for the management of the estate from
the date of the potato failure in 1846. A large sum
was spent in providing meal for the people, and another
large sum in assisting as many as were willing to
emigrate to Canada. I have not beside me at this
moment any note of the exact number who went to
Canada, but in the course of four years it exceeded a
thousand souls. The whole of this was a purely
voluntary emigration, for a great portion of which I
paid the whole cost myself, whilst assisting in the expenses of the remainder. In 1851 the people were still
eager to go, and I print in an Appendix to this paper
the remarkable petition which they sent to me and
to the Government seeking further aid towards emigration. I saw, however, that emigration was not the
only remedy which the condition of the Island required. Active steps were taken to give employment

to the people in draining, in the making of roads, and Measures taken to aid emigration and to give relief and employment to people. in various other agricultural improvements. As the rents of the crofters could not be generally collected, these outlays had to be provided for out of other resources; in fact, I was myself compelled to borrow a large sum; and it is needless to point out that this outlay could not have been provided for at all had the Island belonged to a proprietor depending wholly on its own rental, and still less had it been divided into smaller estates.

Nor did this condition of affairs pass off immediately, or even soon. During the four years from 1846 to 1850 the sum spent on improvements in Tyree and the Expenditure of proprietor in improvements, in addition to sums spent to aid emigration, &c. Ross of Mull was £7919, or, including incidental expenses, upwards of £8000, of which the greater part —about £6373—was in drainage alone. This was in addition to the sums spent in emigration and in the distribution of meal, which could not be repaid either Sir John M'Neill's report to Board of Supervision in 1851. in money or money's worth. In the report of Sir John M'Neill to the Board of Supervision on the Condition of the Highlands and Islands in 1851, he states, from documents then before him, that during the previous four years there had been expended on wages and gratuities to the inhabitants a sum exceeding the whole revenue derived from the property by £4680, which amount, as well as the cost of management, must have been derived from other sources. This is quite true, and is, indeed, a good deal understated. During those years no part of the income derivable from the Island was spent out of it, and the outlays it needed constituted a heavy drain on other resources.

In the year 1851 the reduction of the population

to 3706, and the return of some favourable seasons, brought about the beginning of a better condition of things. But my outlays on improvements, for the sake of employing the people, and for the sake of increasing the produce of the Island, continued to be heavy. In the seven years from the famine to 1851 these outlays exceeded £10,160, of which the greater part was in drainage.

I had by this time begun to find that the outlays on emigration had produced one bad effect—namely this, that the people conceived it to be a boon not to themselves, but only to the proprietor, and were disposed to rely upon him entirely in regard to it. I therefore ceased altogether to offer it to them, leaving it entirely to their own suggestion, although I was always willing to help when occasion required. Sir John M'Neill, in his Report of 1851, mentions that in that year there were 900 persons then anxious to go to join their friends in Canada, from whom good accounts had been received. This number would very nearly have reduced the population to the figure at which it stands at present, that figure being, according to the census of 1881, 2700. It may be roughly assumed, therefore, that the 900 persons who were anxious to go in 1851 represent those who have actually gone from one time to another during the last thirty years.

I may now at once explain to the Commission the principle on which I determined to proceed in the improvement of the Island from the moment when the first extreme pressure of the years of actual destitution had passed away. I was satisfied that the population was excessive, arising from the causes to

which I have referred, and from the ruinous habits
of subdivision which had been inseparable from the
improvidence which is at once the cause and consequence of increasing poverty and of a low standard
of living. Sir John M'Neill points out that the whole
rental of the Island, if divided among its population
even at the reduced figure at which it stood in 1851,
would not have afforded crofts of a higher value than
£4, which is much too small for the subsistence of a
family.

But although I was convinced of the necessity of a
further reduction in the numbers of the people, and
especially of a consolidation of the crofts so that they
should be of a comfortable size, I had an insuperable
objection to taking any sudden step in that direction
such as might be harsh towards the people. I thought
it my duty to remember that the improvidence of
their fathers had been at least seconded, or left unchecked, by any active measures, or by the enforce-
ment of any rules by my own predecessors who had
been in possession of the estate. I regarded myself,
therefore, as representing those who had some share
in the responsibility, although that responsibility was
one of omission and not of commission.

On the other hand, it seemed to me that if, for
the future, rules against subdivision were steadily
enforced, and if every opportunity were as steadily
taken to make good use of the vacancies in crofts
which might arise by death, by migration, and by
emigration, some progress would be made by a slow
but sure process towards a better condition of things.

Accordingly, I determined not only to avoid any- As a rule, no
thing like what has been called a "clearance," but, evictions allowed

except for insolvency or non-payment of rent.

as a rule, not even to allow any individual evictions or dispossession of the existing crofters, except for the one cause of insolvency or non-payment of rent. During the thirty years which have elapsed between 1853 and 1883, there has been only one solitary case of the eviction of a crofter by Warrant of the Sheriff, in the whole Island of Tyree; and this was an eviction made, not in the interest of the Proprietor, but in the interest of the neighbouring tenants.*

Vacant crofts added to others adjacent.

Further, I determined that in all cases when a croft became vacant by any of the causes just mentioned, it should, if possible, not be reoccupied by itself, even when a higher rent could be got by doing so, but should be added to some adjacent croft, if any one of the neighbours was capable of managing and stocking the consolidated possessions.

Farms held by individual tenants kept undivided.

On the other hand, I never contemplated, and could never have approved of cutting up and dividing among crofters the few farms on the island which in 1846 were still held by individual tenants, and all of which had been so held for a long period of time. Most of them had never been possessed by the class of crofters. None of the crofters had capital or knowledge fitting them at that time for the profitable occupation of farms of even a moderate size. The farms held by single tenants were the only farms which afforded any immediate prospect of a great increase of production—they were good cus-

* Certain statements to the contrary on this subject recently made in the press are as false as those made in the same quarter in respect to the occupation of Widows. It is possible, however, that these statements may be due to the ignorance which confounds between forcible evictions and the ordinary "Summonses of Removal," which are issued as a matter of course on all changes of tenancy.

tomers for the cattle of the crofters—and they were the
only field upon which the benefits of good farming could
be held up to the example and imitation of the poorer
people. Tyree is almost singular among the Hebrides in this—that there are no waste lands, properly
so called, upon it. There are no moors—no mosses to
be reclaimed. The old mosses have been long exhausted and cut away to the very bones of rock and
gravel.

No waste lands and no moors on Island.

I wish the Commission, therefore, distinctly to
understand, that with one single exception which I
shall refer to presently, what may be called the large
farms in Tyree have not been gained at the expense
of the crofters. On the contrary, in Tyree the process so much complained of elsewhere has been reversed. The crofters now possess farms which up to
a late date were held by single "Tacksmen;" whilst
in one case only have individual tenants, now occupying the larger farms, replaced the regular crofting
population as it stood in 1846. A few families who
belonged to what may be called the class of squatters,
and who had settled upon one or two of these farms,
occupying upon part of them very small bits of land,
were among the number of those who emigrated, or
were subsequently moved. But with the one exception above-mentioned, the only other example of any
considerable removal of crofters is a case in which
both the cause and the consequences were entirely
different. It arose from insolvency and non-payment
of rent. And in this case the farm was not let to
a new tenant, but was divided between four of the
existing crofting tenants, in respect to whom there
was good hope that with larger and more comfortable

Large farms not gained at expense of crofters.

Case of consolidation of crofts—farm of Mannal.

possessions they would be able to prosper. This hope has not been disappointed. The farm I refer to is the farm of Mannal—formerly subdivided into twenty-three crofts, or rather fragments of crofts, rented at from £5 to 30s. each. This farm is now held by three tenants who have risen from among the rest, of whom two pay rents which place them above the crofting line (£30), whilst the other (a widow) has a croft not much below it (£24, 14s. 6d.).

Explanation as to farm of Hillipol now held by one tenant.

The one exceptional case of a farm now held by a single tenant which in 1847 was held by crofters, is no less remarkable as an illustration of the varieties of circumstance which must determine such results. It is the farm of Hillipol, which had come to be subdivided into twenty crofts so small that one quarter of the whole number were under £2 value, six others were under £3 value, and none exceeded £5 value. In 1847, however, three of them had become vacant and were in my own hands. This was one of the farms on which I determined to expend a large sum in drainage. It was good strong land, but in miserable condition from wet and from the most wretched cultivation. During four years nearly £1000 had been spent in draining and fencing. The tenants had been generally in arrear even at the old rents, and none of them could pay the interest on the outlay, which the land under better management could more than well afford. They naturally fell further into arrear, and were obviously incapable of managing and stocking the farm in its improved condition. The result was unavoidable that during the years of emigration and of insolvency affecting this very poor class of crofts, the tenants of Hillipol were amongst the number of those who disappeared. In 1853 the greater part of the farm was in my own hands. It has since been let as one farm, and it is a signal evidence of the immense increase of production which arises on land well managed, and held by men having sufficient capital, that the rental of this farm has risen from £62 in 1847 to £376 in 1883,—this increase, however, having arisen not without large and renewed outlay on draining and fencing.

The case of Mannal is, I think, a typical case of the process to which we can alone look for the improvement and successful establishment of a class of small farmers. Those who eked out a living between bad farming and bad fishing,—and occasional labour not much higher in quality than the farming or the fishing,—will generally thrive best by pursuing one or other of these occupations by itself, whilst those who are devoted to agriculture can only thrive upon possessions of a certain minimum size. In Tyree generally this result could only be attained upon the principles before explained by a very slow and gradual process. But by that process steadily pursued it has been attained at least to a very considerable extent; and I shall now give to the Commission the figures which indicate that result. *The case of Mannal typical of the only process by which real improvement can be effected.*

In 1846 there were no less than 218 crofts, or bits of crofts, below £5 value. In 1880–81 there were only 34 left of this very poor class. Between £5 and £10 value there were in the same year 102, whereas there are now only 68. On the other hand, the next class, between £10 and £20 value, has been increased and recruited from 38 to 72, whilst the still more comfortable class, between £20 and £50, has been raised in number from 5 to 26, and of these *Present number and value of crofts contrasted with those of 1846.*

no inconsiderable proportion has been lifted altogether above the crofter limit of £30, and the tenants are now ranked among the farmers.

Although I am aware that the special subject of the Commission over which your Lordship presides is the crofter class, it is impossible to consider fully the position occupied by that class (below £30) in any particular locality such as Tyree without taking into account the number of small farms above that line which have been created out of the consolidation of crofts, and are now held by precisely the same class of men, but who have risen by the opportunities which I have thus afforded to them. In connection with this most important part of the objects at which I have aimed I may mention a particular case. A good many years ago advantage was taken of various vacancies to constitute one little farm above the crofting line on the old single farm of Cornaigbeg. In order to complete this possession, and to square off its little fields, it became desirable to get rid of one small croft which stood in the way. It was held by a widow. I desired my factor to offer to her another croft which was vacant, which was quite as good, and was not a hundred yards off. But he had to report to me that nothing could induce the worthy old woman to move, and asked whether I wished him to apply for a summons of removal. I replied that I was most unwilling to take any forcible steps in the matter; but I enclosed a personal letter to the widow explaining the reasons which made me wish that she should exchange crofts,

and assuring her that I did not wish her to be in any way injured by the change. This letter was at once successful, and the widow removed to the croft offered

her in exchange. A very few years later a much larger
farm than that from which she moved became vacant,
and it was advertised to be let. When the offers came in,
I was much surprised to find that my old friend the
widow, who had been so reluctant to move from a small
croft, was much the most eligible offerer for the vacant
farm, and she is now, I hope, comfortably installed in
a possession which is not only far above the crofting line,
but is relatively even a large farm. I do not know any
circumstance which has ever arisen in my management
of Tyree which gave me more pleasure. Last year I
called upon her in her new home, in which I hope she
may be as successful as I wish her to be.

Another case I may mention is one which has
occurred on the farm of Hianish. This farm, when
I succeeded to the estate, was subdivided into six-
teen very poor crofts, most of them below £3 rent,
and only one as high as £6. But this last was held
by a crofter, Niel M'Kinnon, who had given an admir-
able education to a fine family of sons, most of whom
had entered the commercial marine, and one of whom
became highly distinguished as captain of one of the
fastest "Clipper" ships trading to China. The father
died leaving a widow who was justly proud of her
sons, and the late Duchess and I were almost as proud
of her satisfaction in them. In the course of years she
lost them all ; but I have had the great pleasure of en-
larging her croft steadily as vacancies occurred around
her, and of associating with her in the possession her
daughter and her son-in-law, who were alone left
to carry on the succession of a most meritorious
family. I am happy to say that my old friend Widow
M'Kinnon is still alive, and in possession of a little

farm of £50 rental, where I often visit her, and where I trust she and her descendants may continue to be found for many and many a long day.

Case of Farm of Scarnish. Another excellent example is the case of the farm of Scarnish. In 1847 it had come to be subdivided between fifteen tenants—most of them with possessions of the very smallest class—ranging from 20s. to £3 rent. But one of the tenants afforded a nucleus for consolidation, as he already possessed four of the subdivisions, and paid £6, 16s. of rent. But even this small advantage, with a corresponding share of intelligence and of industry, gave to this crofter a start, of which he has known how to take advantage, whilst it has been a pleasure and a satisfaction to me to reward his exertions. As others fell back in the race, he has pressed forward. It has been a regular case—not of the substitution of a stranger but of the promotion of a native. It has been an illustration of the " survival of the fittest." I have lately had the satisfaction of seeing this fine old man—Allan Macfadyen—hale and vigorous at the age of eighty-six— the tenant of the largest part of the whole farm, and sharing it with one other only of the original crofters, who has risen like himself out of that class, and now holds a little farm above the £30 line.

Other cases of improved condition of tenants. There are several other farms on the Island which belong to the same class, ranging above £50 and below £200 a year, and these are all occupied by natives of the Island, who once had much less comfortable possessions. With regard to the old farms of still larger size, which had long been held by individual tenants of the " Tacksmen " class, and had never been subdivided, none of the crofters have had

capital enough to start them, or knowledge to manage
them to the best advantage. Nor has this been Advantage to
otherwise than a great benefit. The jealousy of people of seeing im-
"strangers" coming into such farms is perhaps the mentin agriculture.
most ignorant, if it be the most natural, of all the
Protean forms which the desire of "Protection to
Native Industry" assumes. Nothing tends more
directly to the stagnation of agriculture in such a
distant Island as Tyree than that its people should
never see the example and results of a higher agriculture than that which has been represented by
their own old habits and traditions. The introduction
of new blood is the greatest of all stimulants in such
districts, and without it there would be no advance.

I can specify one signal illustration. The pasturage
of Tyree is particularly rich in clovers, and in grasses
of the most nutritious kind. Consequently it is
admirably and almost specially adapted to dairy-
farming. But dairy-farming was wholly unknown
in the Island until I took pains to introduce it.
The breeding of Highland cattle and of sheep,
together with the growth of potatoes, barley, and
oats, constituted the whole agriculture of the
Island. But when the large farm of Balephetrish
became vacant some twenty-two years ago, I instructed
my factor to look out for a tenant from the low country who should be a dairy-farmer. The disadvantages Introduction of
of residence in a remote Island, the character of dairy farming.
which was little known in the low country, made
this a matter of some difficulty, and involved a very
considerable outlay in buildings adapted for the purpose. But a tenant was found. The experiment has
answered perfectly. The pasturage of Tyree has

proved itself to be admirably and specially adapted to the production of cheese of a high quality, and to the healthy condition of a fine herd of first-class Ayrshire cows. I have had the pleasure lately of renewing the Lease to the son of the tenant who began the enterprise, Mr. Barr of Balephetrish, and who, I have every reason to believe, found it profitable. But this kind of farming, for which the rich and abundant pastures of Tyree are more suited than for any other, is one which cannot be adopted by very small crofters. I am not without hopes that it may be prosecuted, by crofters of the more substantial class, at some future day, when the great care and great cleanliness which are necessary for the production of really good cheese and butter have been established among the people.

Progress among crofters since distress ceased.

I am happy to say that I have seen great progress among the crofters during the thirty years and upwards which have elapsed since actual distress ceased. For a good many years it required stringent rules and regulations to establish anything like a regular rotation of cropping. Nor is this to be wondered at, considering the very short time which had elapsed since their fathers knew nothing better than the old barbarous "runrig" system. The cultivation of the crofts still leaves much to be desired. The little corn-fields are often yellow with weeds. But some turnips are now cultivated, and there are crofts in which a marked improvement has been made on the old traditionary system. I have been lately offering some prizes for the best cultivated crofts, and the judges have informed me that the number of tenants who have done well in this matter has made selection difficult.

These are only special cases, which illustrate the

system I have pursued, and the nature of a process which has produced a marked and steady improve- Distinct improvement resulting in condition of smaller tenants. In direct proportion as the most capable among them tenants. have been selected for the enlargement of their possessions, and as progress has been made towards the establishment of a variety of large crofts and of small farms, the general level of the whole population has been distinctly raised. Some special circumstances Special circumstances favourable affecting Tyree make it more favourable than other to Tyree. districts in the Highlands for small farmers. In the first place, although it is much exposed to gales of wind, and there is comparatively little shelter, yet the climate in other respects is far better than that of the mainland. There is much less rain, the rainfall scarcely exceeding the average of from 35 to 40 inches.* There is also a great deal more sunshine than on the mainland. Snow hardly ever lies. The pastures are naturally very rich. Moreover, the island is admirably suited to poultry, and there is annually a very large export of eggs, amounting, I have reason to believe, to not less than 50,000 dozen. This export represents a revenue to the small tenants from this source alone of at least £1500. The lighter soils produce good barley and excellent oats—crops which are

* I fully expect that "far on in summers which I shall not see" the Island of Tyree will be a great resort for health. Its strong yet soft sea-air—its comparative dryness—its fragrant turf, full of wild thyme and white clover—its miles of pure white sandy bays, equally pleasant for riding, driving, or walking, or for sea bathing— and last, not least, its unrivalled expanses for the game of golf—all combine to render it most attractive and wholesome in the summer months. My own tastes would lead me to add as a special recommendation its wealth of sky ringing with the song of skylarks, which are extraordinarily abundant.

early ripe—and if the sowing were a little earlier than the traditions of the people have made it, the harvests, I believe, would more often avoid the severe gales which not unfrequently do considerable damage. Then, potatoes have often escaped the disease in Tyree during seasons when it was destructive on the mainland, and a few years ago high prices were obtained by the tenants for the seed potatoes which they raised. Lastly, the quality of the cattle, which is one of the staple products of the island, partakes of the superior quality of the pasture on which they feed, and I have endeavoured, by arrangements for the occasional purchase of good bulls, to prevent the decline in that quality, which is very apt to arise among crofters who have not capital to buy in good new stock with sufficient frequency.

General prosperity of tenants. From all these causes combined, I rejoice to say, that during the last thirty years I have had every reason to be satisfied with the small tenants of Tyree. Until quite lately there has been very little arrear, and they have met their engagements honestly. They have been a quiet, sober, industrious, and generally a contented people. I have been accustomed to regard them with some pride and satisfaction, as decidedly superior to others of the same class in most other portions of the West Highlands. During the last two seasons there have been some disastrous gales, an unusually heavy rainfall, and some renewal of the potato disease. But the general prosperity of the tenants has been apparent in everything, and in nothing more apparent than in the comfort of their houses, which are peculiar, and indeed unique in warmth and in solidity among the cottages of the West Highlands. It will be observed that all the articles which Tyree produces, and on which the small tenants depend, are articles in which there has been no depression of prices, but on the contrary a great increase. Wheat is not grown on the island, and wool is an article upon which the crofting tenants do not largely depend in Tyree. Barley, oats, and potatoes have maintained fair average prices for many years, and there has been an immense increase in the price of the class of cattle on which the crofters principally depend. At no time has the price been so high as during the last few seasons. Tyree, therefore, cannot be said to have been exposed to any one of the causes which have produced agricultural depression in other parts of the kingdom. The only special cause injuriously affecting the crofters has been the occurrence of one or two wet seasons, and the occurrence also of some great gales of exceptional violence before the harvest had been secured.

This general conclusion as to the exemption of Tyree from the causes which have elsewhere produced agricultural depression, is a conclusion established by the most conclusive of all proofs, and that is the steady rise in the letting value of land. And this rise has been tested by the simplest and fairest of · all tests—which is the price voluntarily and eagerly offered for the hire of land by farmers of the capitalist class bidding for the larger farms which have been open to competition. It is to be remembered that as regards this class of tenant, the doctrine lately laid down by Sir James Caird* is absolutely and liter-

Exemption from agricultural depression.

Consequent increase of letting value of larger farms.

* In a recent letter to the *Times.*

ally true, that the rent of land is not determined by landlords but by tenants. As regards the small crofters, this doctrine is modified to some extent by the local attachment of a population, which may sometimes be induced to bid above value by the desire or determination to remain where they are even at a sacrifice. But there is no such element in the value set upon land by the capitalist class of tenants, whose action is entirely determined by an intelligent calculation of outlays and returns.

Taking this test, and applying it to seven of the larger farms in Tyree, I find that on these farms the rental of 1847 has been increased by about 220 per cent. The figures are—rental of 1847, £700. Rental of 1883–84, £2260. I need not point out to your Lordship (although it does seem necessary to point out to many other people) what this more than tripling—in some cases the quintupling—of rental means. It means an enormous increase of production. As rent is seldom more than one-third, and is oftener not more than one-fifth of the total produce, the above figures mean that the seven farms in question now turn out at least £6780 worth of human food, instead of food to the value of only £2100.

Great rise of rent quite exceptional.

This great rise of rent is not to be considered as an example of any ordinary increase in the value of agricultural land. I have elsewhere said that the first application of sheep to the mountains of the Highlands was like the recovery of an immense area of country from the sea. It is as stupid to object to it as it would be stupid to object to the drainage of the " Bedford Level." The increase of value which has arisen on some farms in Tyree, consequent on my change of management, is an increase of a similar kind. It did not indeed arise as elsewhere on mountain land, but on land arable and naturally fertile. But it did arise out of a series of operations which have been equivalent to absolute reclamation from utter waste. It is an increase of value measured not only by the height of a new knowledge, but by the depths of a former ignorance. And this is the great lesson to be learned from corresponding increments of value which have arisen all over the Highlands. The squalid wretchedness of the older modes of living and of husbandry, from the want of capital, and of knowledge, and of industry, is the great fact to which it testifies. Such "leaps and bounds" in productive value are not possible in any country where the culture of each generation keeps abreast of the general line of progress in its own day. They are only possible where there have been utter stagnation and positive as well as relative decline. And this was the actual condition of the Highlands during the times I have traced, from an extravagant rate of increase in population, coupled with no increase at all in knowledge, or in capital, or in industry. Hence, when all these conditions began to be reversed, a contrast arose with the former wretchedness which seems incredible. So it has been with the productive power of land in Tyree, where— but only where—the farms could be rendered accessible to modern methods. This is the explanation of the increase of rent upon such farms. It is quite exceptional. It is more like the increase of value which arises on the discovery of a new country. It may almost be said to represent the first advent of civilization in the settlement of a new land. The truth is that under the former system it can hardly be said that the land was cultivated at all. It was simply wasted. The new value is a value both discovered and created. It has arisen from the finding out of adaptabilities unknown before, and from management which has turned these adaptabilities to good account. By that management I have been enabled to realise the prophecy made by Mr. Maxwell of Aros eighty years ago, that the Island of Tyree was capable of producing returns of which the people then "had no conception." The realisation of this estimate has been the combined result of several causes—some of which may be specified:—first, there has been very large outlay by the proprietor in draining, fencing, and building ; secondly, there has been the introduction of a new class of tenant bringing into the Island a new industry, that of dairy farming ; thirdly, there has been the increased facilities of steam communication with the Island—almost comparable with the approach of a new line of railway on the mainland ; fourthly, there has been the great rise in the value of sheep and cattle, and the newly-discovered adaptation of the Island to the production of superior stock and of early lambs ; and last, not least, there has been the substitution of men who prosecute farming as a business for men who simply looked upon a farm as a dignified means of living without the necessity of much skill or the exercise of much activity. Perhaps there has seldom been a case in which we have a more signal illustration of the fundamental value of that old doctrine of the law of Scotland which makes the "Delectus Personæ"— the choice of persons, or the right of choice in the selection of tenants—the most essential of the duties and of the rights of ownership. Without this right, and that intelligent exercise of it which is guided by the most natural and legitimate motives, I am satisfied that there would have been no increase in the agricultural produce of Tyree comparable to that which has actually arisen, and the Island would have remained in a comparatively stagnant, if even it had not fallen into a declining state.

I have brought these facts and considerations under the notice of the Commission because they afford one very good criterion of the justice of any complaints made by the smaller tenants as to the rents they pay. I know of no class of men who deal in the hire or purchase of any article, who would not eagerly testify to any Royal Commission that they would like to get that article cheaper. In respect to no article would such evidence be more eager than in respect to the price of cattle in which these small tenants deal, not as purchasers, but as sellers. The larger farmers, who deal in fat stock, have every cause to feel the stress of the very high prices which they are now compelled to pay to the producers of lean stock. They say that these prices leave them no margin for profit on feeding. The small tenants, however, would hardly admit such an argument as calling for any abatement of the price which the markets afford to them. Yet their own complaints are not more reasonable. Their possessions are really worth double or treble of what they were worth thirty-five years ago. Many of the causes which have led to the rise in the value of land which has been so signally proved in the case of the large farms, have been even more applicable to them.

In particular, the great rise in the value of cattle, and very often of potatoes, they have had the full advantage of. The increased facilities afforded by steam communication have been of equal or even greater value to them in proportion as they have told on the prices of pigs, eggs, poultry, and fish. The breeding and sale of horses have also been a great source of profit—very little considered in the rent. Yet it will be found on comparing the present rental of farms which are still divided into small crofts, with the rental of the same farms as it stood thirty years ago, that the rise of rental has been comparatively small—in some cases quite trifling, and has borne no proportion whatever to the rise in the real letting value of the land as tested by the rent readily obtained for larger farms in the open market,—that is to say, when estimated according to the capabilities of the soil by men with adequate capital who know how to turn these capabilities to full account. The truth is that, if we go back to a still earlier date, such as the years at the beginning of the present century, there has been on some of the farms divided into crofts not an increase but a positive decrease of rent. This has no doubt arisen from the fact that at that time there was some mingling of kelp-rental with agricultural rental, and that when the kelp failed there was some readjustment of rents which were not purely agricultural. The only considerable rise in crofter-rental since 1847 has been on the larger consolidated crofts, and on the small farms erected out of them. It is needless to say that consolidated crofts are always worth a great deal more than the mere sum of their rents when separate. They can be more economically worked, and there is

Rise of rental of small crofts comparatively small.

a much larger proportionate surplus over the cost
of working. This alone accounts for all the rise
of rent which has accrued on the more comfortable
possessions, whilst on many of the smaller crofts the
increase of rent has been almost nominal as compared
with the real increase of value.

Another test of rental may be taken from the careful Test of rental being low.
survey and valuation made in 1771, at which time the
Island was calculated to hold 2488 "soums" of cattle.
This represents the same number of cows, and double
the number of young cattle. Now, as the average
rental of a good Highland cow with its "followers"
upon such pastures is at present about £3, it follows
that the stock fed by the Island of Tyree, without
allowing anything for the improved pastures gained by
drainage, and the improved facilities of management
gained by fences, would represent a rental of £7464
—which is a great deal more than the whole rental
of the Island as it stands at the present moment.
Moreover, it is to be observed that this calculation
excludes all the other produce of the Island—the
sheep, horses, and pigs, the barley, oats, potatoes, and
eggs, which it produces in abundance. Farther still,
it is to be noted that Ayrshire cows have been largely
substituted for Highland cattle, and that one Ayrshire
cow is worth about double the rental which is taken
above as that for a Highland cow. I have reason to
believe that there are in the Island not less than 247
Ayrshire cows, 2155 Highland cattle, 6500 sheep, 651
pigs, and 588 horses. It is curious that this amount
of stock, calculated at rates somewhat below the
market value, and allowing nothing at all for either
horses or pigs, represents a rental almost exactly the

same as the rental calculated on the old "Souming," namely, about £7400.

Perhaps I cannot use a better illustration of the scale of rents in Tyree, than by taking an individual case. It happens to be one of those many widows of whom the agitators have asserted that they are as a rule evicted on my estate. The figures have been supplied to me, not from my own agents, but from a less suspected source. It is the case of a croft rented at a little more than £24. It is now reported to me as holding 7 milk cows, 2 heifers, 8 "stirks," and 40 sheep. This amount of stock at the usual rates would represent a rental of about £31 ; and would unquestionably fetch that rent, and more, if let at the market value.

Result that crofts are held below full value.

Taking all these data together, it seems quite clear that the crofters' lands in Tyree are held generally at rents far below the full value, and such as readily to account for the comparatively comfortable and thriving aspect of the Island and of the people, as contrasted with most other parts of the Highlands which are occupied by a similar class.

Cottars.

Passing now from the crofting and farming population, I wish to bring to the notice of the Commission that in Tyree there is a very large population of mere cottars, some of whom live by fishing, others by labour obtained in the Island, and others again by going to service for some part of the year to the low country. This population may be said, in the language of geology, to be the *detritus* of the old subdivided crofters and sub-tenants. I believe there are no less than about 300 families who live on the Island without paying any rent either to the proprietor or to the

tenants. Some of them are brave, hardy, and successful fishermen, who in some seasons earn a very fair
living, and furnish a very considerable export of salt
fish. The annual average export of salt fish does
not fall short, I believe, of 100 tons—a quantity
which, however considerable (representing not less
than £2000), might be, and I hope will be, much increased. Among the natives of the Hebrides who were
helped to come up to see the late Fishery Exhibition
in London, there were no finer-looking men than some
fishermen from Tyree, and I felt no small pride and
pleasure in their appearance when they called upon
me in London. The harvests of the sea are more
precarious than the harvests of the land. But the
season of 1882 was one of the best on record; and
the price of good salted ling rose to the high figure
of £30 per ton. The fishermen of Tyree labour under
a great disadvantage in the want of any really safe and
commodious harbour. The only natural harbour is
not only a tidal one, but the entrance is very narrow.
On the west side of the Island, which is nearest
some of the best fishing-banks, there is nothing in
the nature of a harbour except some rocky bays, the
entrance to which involves considerable risk in dark
and stormy weather. Yet for many years fishermen
from the East of Scotland have come regularly to
Tyree, and have carried off valuable cargoes of the
finest salt ling. A good many years ago I bought
and fitted out one of the large powerful boats which
are used by these East Country fishermen, and some
good work was done in her by the natives of Tyree
to whom she was lent. Of late, too, I have again
offered to two of my tenants who are enterprising

Some of these are fishermen.

Fishings.

Want of safe harbour.

fishermen a loan to enable them to provide a new boat of the same class; and I hope this may soon be effected. I regret to add that the advice of the most eminent engineers does not encourage me to believe that on the open and stormy shores of Tyree—exposed everywhere to a tremendous surf—it would be possible to construct any really safe harbour at any moderate, or indeed almost at any cost.

Construction of safe harbour difficult, if not impossible.

I have said that the cottar population of Tyree is the *detritus* of the old subdivided crofting population; but I ought to have added that it is also in great measure the remains of the old kelp-burning or kelp-gathering population, which had once been so lucratively employed. And in connection with this subject, I have to relate to the Commission some circumstances which exhibit in a very striking light the fact—too often forgotten—that the wages of the labouring classes generally depend on influences to which they themselves contribute nothing. There are, perhaps, no sources of income so entirely due to the general progress of society, or very often to the brains and inventiveness of other men, as the opportunities of labour. The circumstances to which I refer are these. The kelp trade had entirely ceased long before the potato failure of 1846. A few tons were occasionally bought at a trifling price by some manufacturer in Glasgow, but as any important resource to the population in the earning of wages it had entirely failed. It was under these circumstances that, twenty-one years ago, a copy of the "Pharmaceutical Journal of London" came under my notice, which contained an interesting paper on the products of seaweed. In this paper it was shown, as it seemed to me to de-

Cottars are remains of old subdivided crofting population and principally of old kelp-gathering and kelp-burning population.

Facts as to rise of wages of labouring class.

Origin of the Sea-weed Company.

monstration, that there were very valuable elements in seaweed, which were entirely dissipated and lost by the old native mode of manufacturing kelp. That mode was the burning of the seaweed in open kilns along the sea-shores; and the author of the paper showed that this burning was most wasteful, and that, in particular, almost all the iodine—at that time a most valuable product — was evaporated in the fire. I was so interested in this paper, both in a scientific and in a practical point of view, that I put myself in communication with the author, Mr. C. C. Stanford. I laid before him all the doubts which occurred to me whether the result of experiments on a small scale in the laboratory would be borne out when like chemical operations were required on a large scale, and in respect to so bulky a material as raw seaweed. On his replying to the effect that he was satisfied of the soundness of his calculations, I informed him that I could give him an ample field to work on, the shores of an Island which had once supplied annually from 200 to 300 tons of the old kelp;— that if his calculations were even an approach to the actual results, the profits would be large to him, and would afford once again an important industry to the people. He answered that he was unable to supply the considerable amount of capital which would be requisite, and on this ground alone declined my proposal. A few days later, however, he informed me that he had reconsidered the matter, and thought he could get together a small company which should undertake the experiment. This was the origin of the Seaweed Company, which has since for twenty years effected an important revival of the trade in

seaweed and its products. Continued changes in the
market price of some of these products, arising out
of new mineral sources of supply, have since greatly
deranged the original calculations of Mr. Stanford.
The rent he originally agreed to pay has never been
fully realised, and has now been reduced to an inconsiderable sum. But his processes have not ceased to
furnish employment to a large number of persons,
including women and children, who could not otherwise have had any employment at all. I have been
informed that in the season 1880-1881 the people of
Tyree made no less than 376 tons of kelp, and gathered
no less than 417 tons of " dry tangle," which, at the
lowest calculation, must have dispensed among the
poorest classes not less than between £2000 and
£3000. Whatever may have been the amount of
wages expended by this Company among the working classes in Tyree,—and that amount must in the
aggregate have been very large during the last twenty
years,—the whole of it has been brought to them from
causes to which they contributed nothing. It has
been due, in the first place, to Mr. Stanford's scientific
knowledge and skill. It has been due, in the second
place, to the proprietor's notice and appreciation
of the prospects which Mr. Stanford's experiments
afforded ; and it has been due in the third place to
the proprietary right under which alone Mr. Stanford
could obtain, for his capital and for his riskful enterprise, the requisite security of a Lease. I am glad to
be informed by Mr. Stanford that though the value of
iodine and of potash has been so greatly reduced as
now to afford little profit, there is a prospect that

Employment given by the Company in the Island.

chemical science may discover some products entirely
new which may become valuable.

I regret to observe that some of the people employed Truck system of
complain of the Company resorting to the Truck the Company.
system, and paying wages in kind. I disapprove
much of that system, but I know the extreme
difficulty of abolishing it, especially in remote districts,
where there are no local banks, and where very often
it is for the convenience of both parties that money's
worth should pass as money. I am informed, moreover, that the payments to the people are often made
long in advance of the delivery of the produce, and
partakes largely of the nature of a payment to credit.
In this case there not only is no competition, but there
can be none with the Company, because there are no
other traders in kelp, and no other chemists who de-
vote themselves to the methods of treatment devised
by Mr. Stanford. But it would be much better that
the nominal rate of wages should be reduced and
regularly paid in money.

Before leaving the subject of the cottar or labour- Island unsuited for
ing population of Tyree, I must point out to the Com- maintenance of
people in excess of
mission that in one important matter the Island is number profitably
specially unfitted for the comfortable maintenance of employed.
any excess over the number which can be regularly
and profitably employed. I refer to the total ex-
haustion of the old peat mosses which once existed on
the Island, and which all over the Highlands generally
afford abundant fuel. This resource is wholly wanting in Tyree. There are no peats, and the want of fuel
compels all the people to buy coal, or to resort to such
expedients as the burning of the stalks of weeds, and
even to the destruction of manure by the burning of

dried cow-dung. In some respects this is perhaps hardly to be regretted. The time spent in the Highlands in cutting, drying, stacking, and finally carrying peats, is so great, and the uncertainty of the produce arising from wet seasons is also so great, that peats are often in reality the dearest of all possible fuels, except to people whose time cannot be more profitably employed ; and it may therefore be ultimately an advantage that the people should feel the true cost of living on the Island, as compared with the resources which it affords in the employment of labour.

Management of the Duke's estate in Mull.

Having now explained the general principles on which I have proceeded in the management of Tyree, I may farther inform the Commission that I have acted on precisely the same principles in respect to that part of Mull, including Iona, on which my property had any crofter tenants. I may add, however, that as regards the Ross of Mull especially, the change for the better has been even more marked than in Tyree. But this difference is due to the fact that in the Ross of Mull I started from a still worse condition. The soil and the climate are both inferior to those of Tyree. They are much less adapted to small crofts. Consequently the pauperising results of subdivision were far more conspicuous. In 1846 and the few following years, the aspect of the population, and of the numerous wretched hovels erected by squatting cottars along the roadsides, was most painful. It resembled nothing so much as the descriptions given of the poorest parts of the West of Ireland. The condition of most of the crofters was almost indigent. No less than 102 of them had subdivisions rented below £5, and of these a very large number were under £3 and £2. By the same steady system of consolidation in favour of the most industrious crofters as that followed in Tyree, all this has been completely changed. There are still many crofts which I should like to see consolidated and enlarged. But I have been most unwilling to hasten the process by dispossessing any crofter who could pay his way at all. Progress has consequently been slow. There are, however, now only twenty crofts under £5 value, whilst there are nineteen between £5 and £10. Between £10 and £20 there are twenty-seven crofts, whilst the number of crofts and small farms of the more comfortable class between £20 and £50 has been raised from three to eight. Sums even much larger than those spent on Tyree were spent by me for many years in agricultural improvements on the Ross of Mull, all of which afforded employment to the people—to such of them at least as were disposed to work. The combined effect of all these operations has been a great and visible improvement in the whole aspect of the people as well as of the country. There is no better test than the test of pauperism, or the relation of the poor's rate to the wealth of the community on which it is assessed. The poor's rate, which at one time was the heaviest in the Highlands—about 7s. in the pound— has been reduced to proportions less oppressive to the industry of the ratepayers. It is now only 2s. Well-drained fields, substantially enclosed by some of the finest "Galloway dikes" in Scotland, have replaced spongy mosses and neglected pastures. Wire-fencing on an extensive scale has been erected, and substantial

Visible improvement in aspect of people as well as country.

Test of this improvement in great decrease of poor rate.

D

steadings have been built; so that I question whether in any part of the Highlands agricultural improvement has made more rapid progress.

Expenditure by the Duke on improvements in Mull and Tyree since 1846, £53,610.

To sum up this part of the subject, I may here inform the Commission that my expenditure on improvements, during the period under review, upon the two estates of Tyree and Mull, including Iona, has been no less than £53,610.

Explanation as to increase in Mull rental.

And here I may again point out to the Commission that the increased rental which has been obtained on my estate in Mull during the last thirty-five years has been obtained in the same way, and has been due to the same causes as those which I have indicated in the case of Tyree. As regards all the larger farms, the rents have been determined by the market value offered by tenants who made their own estimate of value, and have had sufficient knowledge and capital to work it out. As regards the crofter class, competition alone has not generally determined rent, but it has been determined by a sort of tariff founded on the value of cattle, and applied to the stock of each croft. Whenever there has been any change of rent, my instructions were to take the stock as rendered by the tenants themselves, to apply to that stock the current rates, and then to deduct at least 10 per cent. from the rent which would be applicable to the larger farms. As the price of store or lean cattle has been steadily rising for many years, and has never been higher than of late, I have every reason to know that the tariff rates applied to that stock are moderate. For example, the rate charged for each milk cow (with "followers" or calves) has been £3, for each two-year-old beast £1, 10s., and for each "stirk," or

one-year-old beast, 10s. For these same classes of
cattle, the prices realised by the tenants last year
have varied from £10 to £14 for the higher class,
from £8 to £13 for the second, and from £3, 10s.
to £7, 10s. for the third.

It is not very easy to compare with perfect fairness
the rise of rent upon crofts and the rise of rent upon
farms. If a farm held thirty-five years ago by one
tenant, and now also held by one tenant, has realised
a large increase of rent, we know that this increase is
due wholly to better management. But in the case
of a farm divided into crofts, a similar rise in rent
would not necessarily mean the same thing. If it
were coincident with a large reduction in the number
of families living on the land, and a consequent consolidation of the holdings, the rise in rent may be
largely due to this circumstance alone. The same
amount of produce, or a comparatively small increase
of it, will afford a larger surplus over the labour spent
upon it, and over the subsistence of the cultivators.
A rent which would be excessive on a farm with a
dozen families living upon it may be far below the
value when these families have been reduced to three
or four—even if there were little or no improvement
in the management. But the consolidation of miserable holdings always does coincide with some degree
of better management, and with some increased production. By itself, therefore, the consolidation of such
crofts is an element in value which is not represented
at all in the case of farms which have always been
held by single tenants. Consequently, when we compare the rise of rent during any given period upon the
two classes of farms, we should allow for this differ-

ence. A given rise of rent without consolidation is equal to a great deal more than the same rise where consolidation is included. The tenant of the single farm pays his increase, whatever it may be, upon the same article. But the tenant of consolidated crofts pays his increase upon a very different, and a much better, article. And yet, in spite of this great difference, it is very remarkable that the class of tenants who, during the last thirty-five years, have got a better article, pay generally a smaller rate of increase than the class of tenants who have got the same article. In other words, the rate of increase in rent upon consolidated crofts during the last thirty-five years has been less—in many cases immensely less—than the rate of increase in rent upon the larger farms. There could not be a better example of this than a comparison between the increase of rent which has arisen upon the Island of Iona and upon a single farm opposite to it upon the shores of the Ross of Mull. There has been considerable consolidation upon Iona, and the tenants on it have had, besides, all the advantages which thirty-five years have brought in the higher prices of produce and in the readier access to markets. Yet the increase of rent on Iona during more than a whole generation has been only 48 per cent., whereas on the single farm of Fidden, on the Ross of Mull, which may be said to be adjacent, the increase of rent has been no less than 158 per cent. Allowing for some special and accidental circumstances in this case, the general result is unquestionably true, that even with the inherent advantages of consolidation, added to all other causes .of increased value which affect equally both classes of possession, the rise on the crofter rental has been generally very far below the rise on the rental of the more substantial farms. There has been great outlay of late in Iona upon fencing, which is the most important of all improvements on land chiefly pastoral. The value of land in Iona has been lately tested in the most satisfactory of all methods—that of the market. A small farm rented at £72 was given up by the tenant, and was open to any other tenant choosing to offer for it. No difficulty was found in re-letting the farm at the same rent to one of the smaller crofters, who is now in possession of it—one of those cases of promotion which always give me the greatest satisfaction.

I now come to the grievances which have been com- *Remarks on evi-* plained of before the Commission in Tyree. And if I *dence given before Commissioners in* approach this part of the subject with some pain, that *Tyree.* pain is much lessened by the strong internal evidence by which I recognise the exotic character of those *Exotic character of* complaints. For the most part they do not belong to *complaints made.* the circumstances of Tyree at all, and are the mere echo of complaints which have been stereotyped elsewhere. One curious illustration of this struck me at once. In Ireland there has been no more fertile source of quarrelling and discontent than what is there called the right of "Turbary." Nowhere in the Highlands, so far as I know, has the privilege of cutting peats been similarly disputed. But the anonymous "factors" *Complaint of de-* who have suggested complaints for the crofters, seem *privation of privi-* *lege of cutting* to have included this in their list. In no other way *peats.* can I account for the fact that one of the crofters of Balemartine, in Tyree, complained before the Commission that he had been prevented from cutting peats. Now it so happens, as I have already explained, that there are no peats in Tyree—the mosses have long been exhausted, and if there is any soil of a peaty nature, it has long been reclaimed, and must now belong to the arable or to the meadow land. If the crofter who made this complaint really meant that he should be allowed to cut up for burning any of the turf on arable, or on meadow, or on pasture land,—whether on his own or on his neighbours' crofts, —he must be unreasonable indeed. The true explanation I take to be that this poor man had learnt his lesson imperfectly, and in repeating what he had heard or read of the right sort of thing to say, he had stumbled on this most inappropriate " grievance."

The complaint, however, may have had another origin, and if it had, we have an excellent illustration of the desire to revert to old habits, however barbarous, which inspires many of these complaints. Some thirty years ago it used to be the custom of the people of Tyree to spend many weeks of the year in cutting, stacking, and drying peats in the Ross of Mull—these peats being then boated across to Tyree at another season. This custom has been abandoned for many years, and for many reasons. In the first place, it involved an enormous expenditure of time and labour. In the second place, it damaged greatly the common pasture of the crofters, who then, as now, occupied the farm on the Ross of Mull on which the mosses lay. In the third place, there was great danger, and not seldom a serious loss of life, in taking boats heavily laden with peats across twenty miles of an open and stormy sea. For all these reasons, and for others, this wasteful habit has been long abandoned by general consent, whilst the improved agriculture

and industry of the people have led them to understand that coal is really cheaper. Yet I think it very
probable that the delegate who made the complaint
had it in his head to revert to this old ruinous
and abandoned mode of procuring fuel. In this,
as in all other matters, the instinct and desire is
to go back from every step of advance in civilisation
and economy which has been taken for the last fifty
years.

But another case is even more remarkable. The Complaint of
delegate who appeared on behalf of three farms, or "eviction" of crofters.
townships, called respectively *Caolis, Salum,* and
Ruaig, is reported to have dwelt on the still more
stereotyped grievance of "eviction"—of crofters sacri-
ficed to "large sheep-farmers," and, of course, also, of
excessive rents. Now, it so happens that these three The three farms
farms are at this moment as exclusively and wholly exclusively
occupied by crofters as they have ever been—that not occupied by crofters.
one single acre has ever been taken from them to
aggrandise any large farm—that not one single eviction unless for insolvency has ever taken place upon
them, and that upon the most assured data of valuation their rents are very far below the rate at which
other parts of the Island, not superior in quality,
have been let, and have been eagerly taken.

This case of a regular formula of grievances "got
up" outside the Island, and put into the hands and
mouths of a simple-minded people, is really so curious
that I must lay it, in some detail, before the Commission.

The three farms of Caolis, Salum, and Ruaig
occupy the whole north and north-eastern end of the
Island of Tyree. They are entirely surrounded by the

sea on three sides, and along their landward boundaries they touch two other farms—Kirkapol and Vaull,—which are wholly occupied by crofters like themselves. Ruaig was one of the farms which, having a shore much exposed to southerly and south-easterly gales, furnished in former days a very large supply of the finest drift or deep-sea seaweed, which made the best kelp. As this kelp was largely credited to the tenants who collected and burnt it, the rent was increased so as to include some portion of the value, and the rental of the farm in 1808 was as high as £320. But this rental had long been reduced to less than one-half, and in 1847 it stood at £150. Up to the end of the last century it was not held by crofters at all, but by a single tenant of the "tacksman" class. It has some excellent strong land, a still larger portion of light sandy soil, some very fine meadow pasture, a good deal of natural shelter among rocky knolls, and a very favourable exposure. In 1808 it had been divided between 16 tenants. In 1847 there were still 15, and at present the number of tenants is reduced to 12. This reduction has been effected upon the plan already detailed —by taking advantage of vacancies as they arose, and consolidating the possessions. One of these crofts is close upon the border-line of £30, and the others range from £8 to £19. I should have selected them as representing a very comfortable class of the Tyree crofters. I was among them last year. I saw some crofts cultivated with neatness and cleanliness decidedly above the average, and not one word of complaint of any kind was addressed to me. If these crofters now complain that their crofts are too small, they have only to select from among themselves those who should make way for the remaining number, and I shall be most happy to consolidate farther the possessions, which I admit are still smaller than I should like them to be. But if they desire to annex any of the crofts belonging to their neighbours on the two adjacent farms of Kirkapoll, and Vaull, I must consult the wishes of those who are to be dispossessed.

The same observations apply to the smaller farm of Salum. The number of crofters has been reduced by the same process from six to four, and of the four who now occupy the farm, one has a croft worth £24 rent, another has a croft worth £19, a third has one of £15, whilst only one has a croft of the £8 class. The third farm, that of Caolis, had twelve crofters in 1847, and has still as many as ten. But of these divisions, one is a little farm of £46 rent, and another is a croft just at the upper limit of the class, namely £30: the other eight vary from £16 to £9. Caolis is in many respects one of the best farms in Tyree. In the report of 1778 I find it described as "a very fine farm already enclosed; the arable of the best quality, and the grass fine pasturing."

The general result as regards these three farms is this: In 1847 the aggregate rental of them all was £356, whilst at the present moment the same rental is £415, showing an increase in thirty-five years of only 17 per cent., whilst similar lands let to larger tenants have advanced, as I have shown, during the same period, by about 220 per cent. The lowness of the rent may be estimated in another way. I find from the detailed report and survey of the farms in 1777, that these three farms

Comparison of rental of these farms in 1847 and now.

have no less than 764 arable acres, besides 256 acres
of meadow, whilst the "souming" of cattle amounts
to no less than 804. It is obvious that after making
every allowance for some land of a light and sandy
character, this great extent of arable acreage and of
meadow pasture—upwards of 1000 acres—capable of
sustaining so large an amount of stock, must be very
moderately rented at £415. This rental is beyond
doubt very much below the rental which these lands
would realise if they were let in farms—still small
—but of a more substantial size; and it exhibits in
a strong light the truth and justice of the complaint
made against my factors that they had "used every
means to exact more rent from them."

Erroneous state-
ments as to half of
Island being sheep
farms. Another indication of the exotic and stereotyped
sources of this complaint from the three farms I speak
of is to be noted in the phrases used about the larger
farms. "The half of the island was under sheep tacks,"
&c., &c., &c. Now it so happens that the only large
farm within several miles of these crofters is not a sheep
farm at all, but the farm on which I have taken so much
pains, and laid out so much money, to constitute a first-
class dairy farm. I refer to the farm of Balephetrish.
But "sheep farms" are the current bugbear of the
agitating agents, and the poor tenants have simply
repeated the stock phrases without the smallest refer-
ence to the local facts. These phrases are all the
more absurd in the present case, since I have good
reason to believe that the very men who use them are
themselves sheep-farmers on no inconsiderable scale—
that is to say, they profit largely by subletting their
land to the larger farmers for the "wintering" of sheep,

a source of profit out of which alone they can meet a good percentage of their whole rent. I am informed that they are able to demand, and do actually receive, for the grazing of a few months in winter, a rent per head of sheep quite as high as that which the proprietor would receive for the whole year.* It is obvious, therefore, that the talk about sheep farms as a grievance is talk quite irrelevant to the circumstances of Tyree. There is indeed one large farm on the Island, the famous "Reef of Tyree," which is chiefly—though by no means exclusively—pastured by sheep. It is a great plain containing about 1000 acres, which has been once covered by the sea, and is still very slightly raised above its level. It is absolutely unfit for tillage, being almost pure sand. Nature fits it for the pasture of sheep and cattle, and for nothing else. It is true, also, that on almost all the rich pastures of Tyree held by the larger farmers, sheep are more or less extensively pastured,—just as they are pastured on arable farms in the Lowlands, and in England,—and are fed and bred for the production of early lambs. But cattle, rather than sheep, are the main produce of the Island ; and as there are no mountains, and only three low elevations on the Island worthy of even

* It is indeed a curious illustration of the utter ignorance which inspires the present outcry against sheep-farming, that, as one of the ramifications of this branch of rural economy, it is now a most important aid to the arable farming of the low country. I was very much surprised to find, quite lately, from one of my own tenants in an arable farm, that he was able to get as much as 9s. per head for the "wintering" of sheep on his fields. This is between two and three times the rent which the proprietor of mountain grazings can get for the same sheep during the whole year.

the name of hills, it is obvious that there is no room for the class of sheep farm to which this phraseology is usually understood as applying. But if the crofters of these three farms refer to the thriving dairy farm of Balephetrish, which is the only large farm within many miles of them, I can only say that they refer to a farm which has never at any time been in the hands of the crofter class, and which they have no more claim to possess than to possess any farm in Lanarkshire or the Lothians.

Complaints suggested to tenants. I lay, however, very little blame to the tenants into whose mouths these irrelevant complaints have been put. When men of that class are exposed to hearing and reading every day one continually repeated and reiterated set of stories, and when belief in these stories is instilled into them by an active propaganda, it is very difficult for them to resist the influence. The result reminds me of what are called in mesmerism "the Phenomena of Suggestion." This result I have myself seen. By very simple means the mind can be thrown into such a state of passive credulity that it will receive and accept everything and anything that it is told, provided only that the tale is repeated with sufficient frequency and with sufficient emphasis. The very senses, though apparently awake, are made to minister to the delusion, and the unfortunate "subject" speaks and acts in a world absolutely different from that by which he is actually surrounded. I have seen a man so influenced, in a room in Princes Street, Edinburgh, made to believe that he was at market, and that a piano in the room was a horse for sale.

Groundlessness of complaints. Possibly something of this nature may account for the dream of the tenants on the three farms in the north end

of Tyree, that they are suffering from "evictions," when
not one has ever taken place ; that their pasture has
been taken from them, when not a single acre has ever
been subtracted from the possessions ; that they are
surrounded by "sheep runs," when they are really
surrounded by crofters like themselves ; and that the
very existence on the Island of a successful dairy farm
is the cause of all evil and of all poverty in the Island.
I have already indicated my opinion on the complaint
against "strangers" being allowed to hold any land.
But the absurdity of this complaint, in the present
instance, may be estimated by the fact that out of
some 220 tenants on the Island there are only two who
are Lowlanders. All the other tenants, including
those who hold the larger farms, are, without exception, Highlanders speaking Gaelic, whilst the vast
majority of possessions, including all the enlarged or
consolidated crofts, are held, moreover, not only by
Highlanders, but by natives of the Island.

I observe that certain of the crofters complained of
some paper or document which they allege they were
required to sign by a former factor some thirty years
ago. Of this document I know as little as the
witnesses themselves. I can hardly say more,
because not one of the witnesses could say that he
had read it, or knew accurately its contents. But the
vague assertions of its nature made by these witnesses
are evidently erroneous, because they convey the
impression that the tenants were to engage to obey
the factor in anything he might desire. This is
absurd and impossible. But I think it is quite
possible that this trumped-up story is simply an im-
perfect and exaggerated recollection of an engage-

Allegations by Crofters as to Factor requiring them to sign docu- ment thirty years ago.

ment in respect to cropping, and other conditions of agricultural management, which at one time was most properly imposed upon the tenants, and was in the highest degree needed by their condition and habits. In all modern leases there are certain stipulations binding the tenant to observe the rules of "good husbandry," and very often these rules are specified with great minuteness. Their one and only object is to prevent waste and the deterioration of the soil. At a time when small tenants were only just rising out of the wretched "run-rig" system, and when the very elements of good husbandry in the rotation of crops were unknown to them, it was an absolute necessity that the tenants should be bound to cultivate according to the rules laid down for them by those who managed the estate. ·Neither thirty years ago, nor at the present moment, can some rules in regard to cropping be dispensed with,—especially in Tyree, where, in addition to all the usual evils of bad management, there is the special and additional danger arising from "sand-blowing." I have very little doubt that the paper referred to by the crofters and of which they have given so apocryphal an account, was a paper of conditions relative to this subject—if, indeed, it ever existed at all.

Groundlessness of complaint about drying seaweed on crofts.

I am almost ashamed to notice one of the complaints brought before the Commission in Tyree, it is so unreasonable ; but I do notice it chiefly on account of a remark which it elicited from one of your Lordship's colleagues. I refer to the complaint of a crofter that the Seaweed Company used his croft for the purpose of drying seaweed upon it. The slightest cross-examination on the subject of this complaint would have elicited facts proving its absurdity. But instead of any such cross-examination, one of the Royal Commissioners, Professor Mackinnon, is reported to have put the following question to the manager of the Seaweed Company :— "That is to say, the Duke takes two rents for the same piece of land—one from you and one from the crofters ?" This implied censure, put in the form of a question, is an excellent example of the sort of claptrap that is now prevalent on all questions connected with the management of land. Upon no other subject—in respect to no other kind of business —would any ear be open to such departures from reason and from common sense. If it were possible for an owner of land to devise a dozen different uses for any part of it, he could only be serving better the public interest in so doing. He could only be meeting the wants of a larger portion of the whole community. Yet Professor Mackinnon seems to think that it must necessarily be an unjust or an injurious thing for a proprietor of land to let it for two or three separate uses to two or three separate persons, each of them paying separately for the particular use which is of value to him. A moment's consideration, or the most elementary knowledge, would have enabled him to recognise the fact that this is a transaction of the commonest kind and of the most perfect equity. It is as just, for example, as that a Professor should charge two separate fees for two separate courses of instruction. If Professor Mackinnon were to give two distinct courses of lectures, one on the Celtic language, and another on the Sanscrit language, and if he were to charge, as he would have the best right to do, two separate fees for these, then two separate rents would be raised from the one piece of brain belonging to Professor Mackinnon. In like manner, it is very common, and quite as just, that proprietors get one rent for the minerals underneath the surface of a piece of land, and another rent for that surface itself. Nor is this all : it is quite common also that the surface, should be let for two or more distinct purposes, each kind of use bearing its own value. Tenants also very often get two or more sub-rents for the same piece of land. It may bring one rent for hay at one season of the year, and another rent for the " wintering of sheep" at another season of the year ; and so on through innumerable varieties of circumstances of which Professor Mackinnon seems to be almost as ignorant as I am of Celtic etymology. But in reality, the particular case of " double rent " which troubled the Professor in Tyree is no case at all. The Seaweed Company does not itself dry the seaweed. It contracts with the poorer crofters and cottars of the Island, according to ancient usage, for collection and drying of the seaweed, and those who take the contract spread out the seaweed, not on the arable land or enclosed fields of the crofters, but on the extensive " links " of common pasture which girdle the shore almost all round the Island. With this usage, which is as old as the trade in kelp—about 150 years—individual crofters who may not happen to have any interest in kelp have no more right to interfere, than with any other condition of custom,— or of use and wont,—under which they have always held their lands. No separate rent is paid to me in respect of this usage ; and besides, it is well known that the spreading of seaware upon pasture, instead of being any injury, is of decided manurial value. Instead of being patted on the back, and encouraged by erroneous comments, the witnesses who made this complaint, ought to have been cross-examined upon it, and when the truth was ascertained it would have been apparent that they deserved rebuke for their selfishness and injustice. For it is quite obvious that if they could prevent this temporary use of the sandy links of Tyree, the real injury would fall mainly upon their poorest neighbours — upon the cottars and upon the smallest crofters of the Island, who are generally the contractors for the collection, drying, and burning of the weed. The Seaweed Company is bound by its lease to compensate for any agricultural damage it may occasion, and if the tenants neither get nor ask for any compensation it is for the very good reason that they could not prove any damage at all. But if this complaint were listened to, very great damage indeed would arise to the most needy of their neighbours. A better example could hardly be given of the manufacture of grievances, and of the use to which the manufacture is put.

I am very sorry that, before passing from the sittings of the Royal Commission on my estate, I should find myself under the necessity of referring to a matter which, though primarily affecting individuals only, is nevertheless a matter of real public interest. I deem it to be my duty to complain of certain questions which were addressed to my chamberlain, Mr. Wyllie, by one of your Lordship's colleagues, Mr. Fraser Mackintosh. " Is it, or is it not, the chief duty of a chamberlain to raise rents ? " is one of those questions,

Questions put by Mr. Fraser-Mackintosh to Mr. Wyllie, the Duke's chamberlain.

E

as given in the reports. The intelligence of this question is on a level with its courtesy. Factors are very often the suggesters and almost always the surveyors of agricultural improvements. In this respect I know of no one class, equally limited in number, which has contributed so largely to the wealth of the community. But except in this way, the rise in value of all the larger farms on my property—as elsewhere in Scotland generally—has been due to causes as independent of factors as it could have been independent of Doctors or of Attorneys. Even as regards the crofts, their rents have been determined on a tariff whose ultimate basis is the price of cattle and of other produce, as well as the offers of the people themselves for vacant possessions. There is no temper of mind so illiberal as that which dictates such sneers against a whole profession. Mr. Fraser Mackintosh's insinuation against Mr. Wyllie is as unfounded as it was offensive. I can say with absolute truth that in his advice to me, as well in the matter of the valuation of land as in all others respecting the management of my estate, I have always found that spirit of justice and moderation which are so conspicuously absent in the treatment he himself received.

But Mr. Wyllie was not the only object of invidious insinuation. For I have further to observe that this same member of the Royal Commission, not content with making unjust accusations against a gentleman who is alive, thought proper to suggest accusations still more gross against another gentleman who cannot now answer for himself. In questioning another witness,—a crofter who could not possibly know anything of the matter,—Mr. Fraser

Mackintosh made suggestions in respect to my late factor, Mr. Campbell of Ardfinaig, which admit of no other interpretation than this—that he may have produced to me false vouchers for an expenditure on improvements which was never really laid out.* I will not stop to refute such an accusation by explaining my own habits of business, or my own personal inspection during many years of the improvements which were made. I understand that the Commission landed from a steamer at the village of Bunessan, and re-embarked without having time to see anything whatever of the estate. And, indeed, even if the present condition of the country- had been examined no judgment could have been arrived at on the subject of improvements without a recollection of its previous condition thirty-five years ago, and a comparison between the two. It is impossible, therefore, that any member of the Commission could be possessed of any of the data on which alone an expression of incredulity could be justified as to the facts of my outlay, stated by Sir John M'Neill in his Report of 1851, or as to the integrity of the gentleman under whom that outlay, and still greater subsequent outlays, were expended. I need not farther indicate what every just mind must think and feel of the moral character attaching to such insinuations—when it is not even pretended that they are based on a particle of evidence. It is true that there is no law of libel open

* The question I refer to is thus reported : "May not this large sum of money that has been mentioned have gone out of the Duke's pocket, and yet never been expended on the estate ? Is it quite possible that documents, stamped papers, things of that sort, may have been presented to the Duke, showing that the money had been all spent on the property ? "

to the dead,—nor even, I am afraid, to their kindred who are alive. Possibly also the position of a Royal Commissioner might be privileged. But, if so, the privilege carries an obligation which is all the more binding. I wonder whether it ever occurred to Mr. Fraser Mackintosh to ask himself whether Mr. Campbell has no relatives who may be wounded, but who may have no redress. Mr. Fraser Mackintosh seemed eager to take under his protection the widows on my estate whom it had been falsely reported that I have been in the habit of dispossessing. Did it ever occur to him to ask whether Mr. Campbell had left a widow, to whom his imputations of fraud against her husband would have been a bitter trial? Such a widow there was,—one of the best women I have ever known,—a woman of the highest Christian character—under whose roof I have spent many happy hours when examining improvements on the estate, and through whom the late Duchess was long accustomed to dispense her charities for the poor of the Ross—feeling and knowing that they would be distributed with sympathy and with personal knowledge. Within the last few weeks I have heard her name—and her husband's name too—mentioned with grateful remembrance among the really poor on the Ross of Mull. She is now dead ; but she died only a few short months ago ; and much as I felt the death of an old friend so closely associated with former days, I am now thankful that she was removed in time to escape the great pain which would undoubtedly have been inflicted upon her by the shameful insinuations against her husband which were conveyed in the words of Mr. Fraser Mackintosh.

I hope no one will think that I look upon your Lordship as needing any words of mine to impress upon you the true character of such questions as that to which I have referred, and as others to which you have, only too often, been compelled to listen. The dignified courtesy with which your Lordship has treated all who came before you makes any such interpretation impossible. But reckless charges — and sometimes the dissemination of disproved accusations against both the dead and the living—have been so much a regular part of the recent agitation, that I hold it a public duty to animadvert upon any conspicuous exhibition of the same tendency.* In the case of the questions to which I have referred, even your Lordship's great patience was broken down ; and I rejoiced to observe the severe censure which was implied in your interruption of your colleague, and in your public announcement to him that you "cannot allow questions of that character."

Looking back at the principle on which I have conducted the management of my estates in the Islands during the last thirty-five years, I am satisfied of its soundness. I am glad to see that one of the witnesses,† himself a crofter, testified to the greater comfort of those who hold consolidated possessions. I am not less glad to see that another witness ‡ testified to the favourable accounts received of those

Soundness of principle on which Duke's estates have been managed.

---

* An excellent pamphlet lately published by Mr. Sellar refuting certain calumnies against his father in respect to the Sutherland removals exposes, as they deserve to be exposed, the authors of some recent books which have revived against the dead accusations refuted at the time before a judge and jury.

†·Lachlan M'Phail, Kilmoluaig (rent payable jointly with another £49).

‡ Dr. Buchanan.

who have emigrated to Canada. It is something in
this inquiry to have even the most palpable truths
admitted and not denied. Changes which benefit
both those who go and those who remain cannot be
changes for the worse. But there is something more
to be said than this. It is literally true that if there is
now any comfort or substance among the crofters of
Tyree it is entirely due to the system I have pursued.
If, on the other hand, there is any poverty remaining
among them, it is due to the restraints upon the
execution of that system which sentiment and feeling
have imposed upon me. I have avoided to the utmost
all gratuitous evictions, or even removals, and yet
there is hardly a single crofter in Tyree who has not
had the size of his possession doubled or trebled during the last thirty-five years. Every one of them
has profited more or less largely by the departure of
his neighbours, and generally by the system against
which a few of them have now been incited to
grumble or object. Hardly a single croft remains
of what may be called the old pauperising class,
although many are still much smaller than I should
wish them to be. A new proprietor, as all observation proves,* would have applied the principle

* On no part of the subject has greater nonsense been written
and spoken than on the connection of the old law of entail with
what is called the " Crofter question." The law of entail may be,
and was, open to many objections. But it was eminently favourable to crofters. It is almost invariably on the estates of the old
families that the crofters have been retained. It is almost as
universally from the estates of new purchasers that they have disappeared. This fact could not be better illustrated than by
comparing the lands in Mull and Morvern which were sold by the
Argyll family at the beginning of the present century with the
lands which still belong to me.

of consolidation much more rapidly, and would perhaps have attained even greater results, as regards increase of produce, in a much shorter period of time. But I have been content to allow natural causes to operate, and to let time and experience prove the unavoidable conditions of insolvency which attach to the improvident subdivisions of land. Setting aside the case of allotments for men living mainly on the wages of labour or on handicrafts—which belong to a wholly different category—I am opposed to the system of very small crofts, as I am equally opposed to the system of farms enormously large. My aim has been to consolidate the small crofts gradually, as the vacancies by death and insolvency arose, not into farms of great size, but into farms of a variety of sizes. And the general result of my operations is at least as near an approximation towards this end as has been compatible with my desire to avoid harsh or hasty proceedings of any kind.

Gradual consolidation of small crofts.

The proper size of farms is essentially a local question, depending very much on the conditions of physical geography. A very large part of the Highlands consists of high mountains, many of them having no arable land at all even upon their flanks. The only agricultural value of these is as grazings for sheep. The capital required for adequately stocking them is always comparatively large. Flocks of two and three thousand sheep represent large sums of money. This capital is entirely beyond the reach of men who have never held anything but crofts or small farms. I have no belief in the success of the co-operative management of such grazings. Common grazings are the subject of perpetual quarrelling, even

Proper size of farms a local question.

Common grazings unsuitable.

when tried on the small scale common to old townships in the Highlands ; and even when peace is kept
and quarrelling avoided, it is done only by the sacrifice of that spirit of individuality in enterprise and
improvement which is the life and soul of all in-
dustrial pursuits. The quality of the stock on such
joint possessions is generally and notoriously inferior. The higher mountains, therefore, of the
Highlands must always continue to be held in
comparatively large farms. But there is another
large area of the Highlands which consists of hills
of smaller elevation, with a mixture of slopes and
hollows of arable land, and sometimes with very considerable stretches of level ground between them, which
has been reclaimed or is reclaimable. This is the area
most favourable for small farms, and the great bulk of
the whole area of the county of Argyll is actually so
held. On my own estates even the great mountain
pastures are all held in farms, the value of which is
small compared with the really large farms of the Lowlands of Scotland. In illustration of this fact let me
direct the attention of the Commission to the farming divisions upon my own estate in the Island of
Mull. That estate includes Ben More, one of the
higher mountains of Scotland, and which, with all its
spurs and outliers, is pure grazing land, with no more
than mere fragments of arable soil at a few points
around its base. Yet this great extent of mountain
grazing is held in divisions, the very largest of which
would represent a comparatively small farm in the
Lothians and in many other parts of the Low Country.
There is one farm of £700 ; another of £600 ; a third
of £394 ; a fourth of £219 ; a fifth of £115. Pass-

Higher mountains
must be held in
large farms, but
lower hills and
arable land
adapted for small
farms.

Illustrations in
farming divisions
upon Duke's estate
in Mull.

ing to the Ross of Mull, which belongs to the less
mountainous and more varied area of the Highlands,
the farming divisions exhibit a still more remarkable
example of a great variety in the size of possessions. The maximum rent of any one is only £500.
Between that rent and £300 there are three farms.
Between £300 and £100 there are no less than eight
farms, of which one-half are less than £200. Between
the line of £100 and the crofting line of £30 there are Number of
seven farms; whilst as regards the crofting class itself, crofters.
I have already shown that its status and condition has
been immensely raised and improved. In 1847 the
estate was crowded with possessions below the £5
line, on which it was impossible to maintain a family
in comfort, even if the land had been rent free. The
crofts have now been all doubled, and many have been
trebled and quadrupled in size, some of them having
been thus lifted altogether out of the crofting class into
the class of small farms. As regards the cottars, I see Cottars.
that some of the crofters complained to the Commission that the cottars had cottages upon their land.
But this has always been so, and the continuance of
the fact has arisen from the extreme reluctance I
have always had to evict even cottars if they could
possibly maintain themselves by labour. When,
however, it was asserted by some witnesses that
poverty has increased, I observe with some surprise
that not a single question was put to the witnesses for
the purpose of bringing this assertion to some definite
test. One well-known test is to be found in the
poor's rate; and when I mention that in the parish
which contains the Ross of Mull this rate has fallen
from seven shillings, which was the rate at one time,

to two shillings in the pound, which is the rate now, I have said enough to show how unfounded is the statement as to increasing poverty.

With two exceptions all the farms held by Highlanders.

I rejoice to be able to add that although I object strongly to the exclusion of "strangers" from the possession of farms, especially when they bring new knowledge and new skill into remote and backward districts, yet, as a matter of fact, all my farms in Mull and Iona, with only two exceptions, are held by Highlanders.

Every step towards improvement during last 130 years has been taken by Proprietor and not by people.

Before concluding this paper I think it not unimportant to point out a fact which has struck me much in reading the old documents to which I have referred, and that fact is this,—that every single step towards improvement which has been taken during the last 130 years, has been taken by the proprietor and not by the people. And not only so, but every one of these steps, without exception, has been taken against the prevailing opinions and feelings of the people at the time. "All in this farm very poor and against any change"—such is the description repeated over and over again in a detailed report on each farm sent to my grandfather in 1803, when he was contemplating those changes which were then absolutely necessary. Great poverty and great ignorance are always "against any change." They are invariably associated with a languor of mind which is incompatible with the possibility of improvement. The very desire of better things is absent—and even if the desire existed the means would still be wanting. Under such conditions every reform must begin outside the people and absolutely requires to be pressed upon them. I am not speaking merely of the outlays of money which come from capital. I am speaking of

those exercises of authority which come from ownership
and cannot be enforced without the possession of the
rights of property. The abolition of the run-rig system
was always most unpopular in the Highlands. In
Tyree, as elsewhere, it was abolished, and could only be
abolished by the authority of ownership. Every subsequent measure of improvement—the regular division
of individual possessions,—the fencing of them,—the
selection of the best candidates for the holding of them,
—the building of a better class of houses,—the introduction of ploughs in substitution for the old barbarous
" crooked spade,"—the introduction of carts,—of grain
of a better kind,—of superior stock,—of dairy farming ;
—in short, every item of progress in agriculture has been
the work, and often the arduous and expensive work, of
the proprietor. Moreover, even all these would have
been useless without the arrest laid upon subdivision,
and the steady progress made towards the establishment by consolidation of more adequate and comfortable possessions. If a higher standard of comfort has
now been attained, and if a higher standard of intelligence has followed it, this happy result has been due
entirely to the causes I have indicated. The tendency
to subdivide is now, indeed, checked amongst the
larger crofters, but it has not been eradicated in the
class which still represents, in a mitigated degree, the
former condition of things. It is curious under what
shifts and disguises—sometimes under what accidents
of mere laziness—the old tendency is liable to re-
appear. Some cow is said to want a byre. The byre
is built, and in a short time the cow is expelled, and
a new family is installed instead. I need not point out
that nowhere in the Low Country, or indeed in any

civilised part of Europe, would this process of squatting and subdivision be allowed by the proprietors of land. It is not easy to see why estates in the Highlands of Scotland should be subject to a practice so ruinous to agriculture and so inevitably productive of a pauper population.

Explanation as to present tenancy of Lismore. I have yet to mention one other portion of my estates in the Islands which has been visited by the Commission, I mean a property which belongs to me in the Island of Lismore. I am all the more glad to do so as it affords me an opportunity of pointing to a practical illustration of the views which I entertain as to the varieties of local circumstance which ought to determine the size of possessions. I have no hesitation in saying that my property in Lismore is one of the few cases I know in which consolidation has been carried much too far. But I am not responsible. I purchased the property only a few years ago, and found almost the whole of it under lease to one sheep-farmer, whose ordinary residence and whose largest farms are in the Low Country. Lismore is essentially an island adapted to small farms of mixed arable and pasture. Being wholly composed of limestone, its grazing is magnificent, and there are sheets and patches of arable land interspersed among the hills and rocks, consisting of a soil so rich that Dr. Voelker, the eminent chemist of the Royal Agricultural Society of England, reports to me that it resembles nothing so much as some of the finest soils of the American continent. I can only say that if I live to see the expiry of the present Lease under which the greater part of that property is held, it is my hope and intention to break up the large single sheep-farm, and to divide it into smaller but still comfortable possessions. I believe it to be admirably adapted for dairy-farming, and for the growth of the finest oats and turnips. It has abundant shelter although it has little or no wood. This arises from the steep faces and sudden knolls into which the limestone strata have been thrown, amidst the intricacies of which cattle and sheep can always find spots sheltered from all winds. The island is close to a growing market in the town and port of Oban; and from the splendid panorama of sea and mountains by which it is surrounded, as well as the excellent trout-fishing which it affords, I am not without hope that in summer and autumn, at least, it may have some market from health-seekers within its own attractive shores. In vision at least, if not in fact, I already see it both better peopled and better cultivated. Economic causes of the same kind will operate in the same direction in some other parts of the Highlands where the difficulty of letting to advantage the very large class of sheep farms is already telling in favour of smaller possessions.

I am,

Your Lordship's obedient Servant,

ARGYLL.

Inveraray, Oct. 1, 1883.

APPENDIX.

PETITION from Poor Persons in Tyree for Aid to Emigrate.

Unto Sir JOHN M'NEILL.

The Petition of the undersigned Cottars and small Crofters on the Island of Tyree,

Humbly sheweth,

That since the making of kelp ceased, and particularly since the failure of the potato crop, the inhabitants of this island have been in a state of great destitution ; and, were it not for the benevolence of the proprietor, and the aid afforded by the relief board, they would inevitably have starved. That hitherto they have been employed by the proprietor at drainage and other works, during the winter and spring months, before the land was cropped, and during the summer they were supported by the funds of the relief board. That this latter resource being now at an end, your petitioners' prospects, on looking forward to the ensuing summer, are in the extreme dismal, and the more so, as the only prospect of ultimate relief to which they so fondly cling is denied them—that of emigration— which your petitioners neglected to take advantage of while in their power, probably supposing that the relief funds were to last, or that the potato would be restored. That, to add to their further grievance, your petitioners are led to understand that those adverse to emigration from the West Highlands are using every possible means to prevent it, and that statements are made publicly that the poor can be supported by employing them in the improvement of waste land. Those who advocate such are certainly actuated by other motives save that of philanthropy, and display the grossest ignorance as to the resources of the country, particularly as regards this isolated island, where there is no fuel, and not an inch of waste land which the inhabitants could not drain and trench in a few months. That your petitioners would now most early request, that if possessed of the bowels of compassion, such as were your fore-fathers, or value the lives of your countrymen, you will not credit the statement of those inimical to our best interest, but examine individually into our circumstances, and the condition of the island, when they have no doubt you will have sufficient proof afforded of the fallacy of such statements, and the injury and cruelty done us by such misrepre-sentations, which may perhaps be the means of the Duke's withholding his bounty, and depriving us of the power of participating in the enjoyments and comforts, they are from day to day informed, their friends in Canada enjoy to such an extent.

May it therefore please your honour to take the miserable condition of your petitioners into con-sideration, and use your influence with Her

Majesty's Government, or His Grace the Duke
of Argyll, to provide for them the means of
emigrating; and your petitioners shall ever
pray.

Residence.	Name.	Crofter or Cottar.	Rent.			Number of Family.
			£	s.	d.	
Balinoe	Donald M'Donald	Crofter	3	12	0	8
Burapoll	A. M'Innes	do.	12	0	0	14
Balephuil	C. M'Millan	Cottar	...			9
Balemartin	H. M'Donald	do.	...			8
Balephuil	J. Campbell	do.	...			13
Balemartin	A. M'Lean	do.	...			6
Moss	Hugh Lamont	do.	...			7
do.	A. M'Donald	do.	...			8
Burapoll	J. Carmichael	do.	...			3
do.	P. Carmichael	do.	...			7
do.	N. M'Innes	do.	...			4
Moss	J. M'Donald	do.	...			8
Burapoll	D. Burrer	do.	...			9
Bolinieanach	Mary Brown	do.	...			3
do.	J. M'Lean	Crofter	5	10	0	6
Boliphuil	A. M'Kinnon	do.	1	12	6	9
do.	A. Campbell	Cottar	...			10
Burapoll	A. Lamont	do.	...			6
Hilipoll	A. M'Arthur	Crofter	2	10	0	11
Comoig-beg	L. M'Kinnon	do.	5	2	0	9
do.	L. M'Lean	Cottar	...			2
Kennory	A. M'Donald	do.	...			1
do.	John M'Donald	do.	...			7
Moss	C. M'Lean	do.	...			8
do.	J. M'Donald	do.	...			4
do.	J. Ferguson	do.	...			8
Hilipoll	H. M'Lean	Crofter	1	11	0	3
Comoig-beg	H. M'Lean	Cottar	...			2
Moormal	A. M'Neill	do.	...			6
do.	D. Brown	do.	...			2
Boliphuil	D. M'Lean	Crofter	7	18	0	10
do.	J. M'Donald	do.	6	0	0	2
do.	M. M'Donald	do.	2	0	0	6
Moss	Mary M'Lean	Cottar	...			2*
Baliphuil	A. M'Kinnon	Crofter	4	16	0	13
do.	D. M·Millan	Cottar	...			4
do.	M. M'Millan	Crofter	2	10	6	11
do.	M. Black	Cottar	...			4
do.	Cue. Black	do.	...			3
do.	D. M'Lean	Crofter	3	0	0	8
do.	J. M'Lean	Cottar	...			3
do.	J. M'Lean	Crofter	1	0	0	2

* Pauper.

F

Residence.	Name.	Crofter or Cottar.	Rent.			Number of Family.
			£	s.	d.	
Bolimorton .	N. M'Millan . . .	Cottar	...			7
do. .	J. M'Donald . . .	do.	...			7
Comoig-more	D. M'Farlane . . .	do.	...			4
Hilipoll . .	A. M'Donald . . .	do.	...			1
do. . . .	N. M'Intyre . . .	do.	...			2
Ruaig . . .	J. M'Lean	do.	..			8
Comoig-more	H. Lamont . . .	do.	...			4
Moss . . .	D. Cameron . . .	do.	...			8
Kilmoluaig .	L. Cameron . . .	do.	...			6
do. .	J. M'Lean	do.	...			5
Bolirullin . .	A. Kennedy . . .	do.	...			4
do. . .	L. Black	do.	...			3
do. . .	Christᵘ· M'Lean . .	do.	...			2
Boliphuil . .	D. Brown	Crofter	3	0	0	4
Salem . . .	F. M'Kinnon . . .	Cottar	...			9
Vaul . . .	S. M'Phaden . . .	Crofter	3	15	0	6
Boliphuil . .	A. Kay	Cottar	...			10
Golt . . .	D. M'Kinnon . . .	do.	...			6
do. . . .	H. M'Lean . . .	do.	...			12
do. . . .	A. Brotton . . .	do.	...			5
Mannol . .	N. M'Lean . . .	Crofter	1	7	6	7
Comoig-more	N. M'Phael . . .	do.	6	0	0	6
do.	J. M'Phail . . .	do.	4	14	0	9
Comoig-more.	A. M'Phail . . .	Crofter	6	0	0	4
Bolimorton .	J. M'Arthur . . .	Cottar	...			8
do. .	A. M'Donald . . .	do.	...			3
Kilmoluaig .	M. M'Donald . . .	Crofter	4	0	0	9
do. .	C. M'Intyre . . .	Cottar	...			8*
do. .	C. Cameron . . .	do.	...			5
do. .	N. M'Lean. . . .	do.	...			6
do. .	D. Cameron . . .	Crofter	4	0	0	8
Golt . . .	N. M'Lean	Cottar	...			8
Boliphuil . .	H. M'Phaden . . .	do.	...			11
Vaul . . .	D. M'Kinnon . . .	Crofter	9	0	0	6
Lolt. . . .	H. M'Kinnon . . .	do.	2	0	0	9
Kirkapoll . .	A. M'Lean	Cottar	...			7
do. . .	Christian M'Lean .	do.	...			3
Coales . . .	N. Clark	Crofter	13	0	0	9
Ruaig . . .	D. Clark	do.	12	0	0	8
Coales . . .	D. M'Phaden . . .	Cottar	...			8
Bolirullin . .	M. M'Kinnon . . .	do.	...			6
Coales . . .	H. M'Arthur . . .	do.	...			5
do. . . .	L. M'Donald . . .	do.	...			3
Vaul . . .	N. M'Donald . . .	do.	...			4
Coales . . .	J. M'Donald . . .	do.	...			6
do. . . .	N. M'Phaden . . .	do.	...			3
do. . . .	A. M'Donald . . .	Crofter	12	13	0	8
do. . . .	D. Brown	Cottar	...			7
do. . . .	H. M'Donald . . .	do.	...			5
do. . . .	N. M'Dougall . . .	Crofter	10	0	0	8
Golt. . .	H. M'Millan . . .	do.	4	4	0	11

* Pauper.

Residence.	Name.	Crofter or Cottar.	Rent.			Number of Family.
			£	s.	d.	
Bough . . .	Christian M'Kinnon	Cottar		...		6
Vaul . . .	J. M'Donald . . .	do.		...		4
Ruaig . . .	J. M'Lean	Crofter	10	0	0	4
do. . . .	H. M'Lean . . .	Cottar		...		3
Vaul . . .	J. M'Kinnon . . .	do.		...		2
Heanish . .	D. Sinclair. . . .	do.		...		5
Salem . . .	D. McPhaden . . .	do.		...		4
Heanish . .	C. M'Donald . . .	do.		...		9
Coales . . .	J. M'Lean	Crofter	6	0	0	9
Heanish . .	M. M'Donald . . .	Cottar		...		7
Scourish . .	A. M'Lean	do.		...		5
Comoig-more	D. Campbell . . .	do.		...		1
Kilkenneth .	M. M'Kinnon . . .	Crofter	3	18	0	9
Boliphuil . .	N. M'Donald . . .	Cottar		...		8
Bolimorton .	H. M'Lean . . .	do.		...		7
Coales . . .	R. M'Armoil . . .	Crofter	9	0	0	11
Comoig-more	Marion Campbell .	Cottar		...		4
Moss . . .	Effy M'Lean . . .	do.		...		2
Balmoluaig .	D. M'Phail . . .	do.		...		5
Bolimorton .	Flora M'Phail . .	do.		...		3*
Coales . . .	D. M'Phaden . . .	do.		...		4
do. . . .	D. M'Larty . . .	do.		...		6
do. . . .	A. M'Donald . . .	do.		...		5
do. . . .	Mary M'Larty . .	do.		...		4
Greenhill . .	M. M'Cail	do.		...		5
Boliphuil . .	C. M'Donald . . .	Crofter	3	0	0	8
do. . .	M. M'Phaden . .	do.	3	0	0	6
Moss . . .	J. Cameron . . .	Cottar		...		5
Bough . . .	C. M'Phail . . .	do.		...		8
do. . .	D. Durach	do.		...		6
Hilipoll . .	N. M'Kinnon . . .	Crofter	1	10	0	8
Heanish . .	N. M'Donald . . .	Pauper		...		1*
Comoig-more	A. M'Phael . . .	Cottar		...		3
Kilmoluaig .	C. M'Lean . . .	do.		...		5
Comoig-beg .	H. Brown	do.		...		1
Hilipoll . .	D. Cameron . . .	do.		...		1
do. . .	M. Brown	do.		...		2
Kilkenneth .	Mary Cameron . .	Crofter	0	18	0	8
Balimorton .	N. M'Phaden . . .	Cottar		...		7
Heanish . .	N. Sinclair . . .	do.		...		8
do. . .	D. M'Intyre . . .	do.		...		6
do. . .	N. M'Donald . . .	do.		...		7
Ruaig . . .	N. M'Innes . . .	do.		...		11
						825

* Pauper.

(Signed) JAMES MACFARLANE,

Witness to the above signatures and marks.